Pillsbury family christmas

COOKBOOK

Pillsbury family christmas COOKBOOK

Celebrate the Season with More Than 150 Recipes,
Plus Fun Craft Ideas

By The Pillsbury Editors

Clarkson Potter/Publishers
New York

Home of the Pillsbury Bake-Off®

Pillsbury

*Our recipes have been
tested in the Pillsbury Kitchens
and meet our standards of easy
preparation, reliability and great taste.*

For more great recipes, visit www.pillsbury.com.

Published by Clarkson Potter/Publishers,
New York, New York
Member of the Crown Publishing Group,
a division of Random House, Inc.
www.crownpublishing.com

Printed in Japan

Design by Caitlin Daniels Israel

Library of Congress Cataloging-in-Publication Data
Pillsbury family Christmas cookbook : celebrate the season with more than 150 recipes, plus fun craft ideas.
1. Christmas cookery.   2. Entertaining.   I. Pillsbury Company.
TX739.2.C45P55   2004
641.5'686—dc22   2003027603

ISBN 1-4000-5338-2

10 9 8 7 6 5 4 3 2 1

FIRST EDITION

CREDITS

FRONT COVER PHOTOGRAPH: Christmas Cutouts, page 200; Spiced Walnut Brittle, page 218; Peppermint–Bark Hearts, page 221

BACK COVER PHOTOGRAPHS, CLOCKWISE FROM TOP LEFT: Honey-Mustard Roasted Chicken and Squash, page 126; Almond Baby Carrots, page 143; Deviled Lobster Tails, page 134; Teriyaki Seafood-Stuffed Mushrooms, page 30

FRONTIS PHOTOGRAPH: Individual Lemon–Lime Cream Tarts, page 180

PAGE 6: Pepper-Crusted Prime Rib with Zinfandel Sauce, page 113

PAGE 8: Almost-Instant Buckeyes, page 222

GENERAL MILLS, INC.
Director, Book and Online Publishing: Kim Walter
Manager, Book Publishing: Lois Tlusty
Editor: Heidi Losleben
Recipe Development and Testing: Pillsbury Kitchens
Photography by General Mills Photo Studios and General Mills Image Library, except as noted: pages 16–17, Andre Gallant/Getty Images; pages 44–45, Romilly Lockyer/Getty Images; pages 70–71, Yellow Dog Productions/Getty Images; pages 106–7, Josef Fankhauser/Getty Images; pages 138–39, Andrew Sacks/Getty Images; pages 164–65, Arthur Tilley/Getty Images; pages 198–99, Arthur Tilley/Getty Images; pages 226–27, Christopher Bissell/Getty Images; pages 244–45, Andy Whale/Getty Images.

CLARKSON POTTER/PUBLISHERS
THE CROWN PUBLISHING GROUP
President and Publisher: Jenny Frost
Senior Vice President and Publisher: Lauren Shakely
Editor: Rosemary Ngo
Editorial Assistant: Laura Motta
Creative Director: Marysarah Quinn
Designer: Caitlin Daniels Israel
Managing Editor: Amy Boorstein
Associate Managing Editor: Mark McCauslin
Senior Production Editor: Sibylle Kazeroid
Production Supervisor: Linnea Knollmueller
Director of Publicity: Tammy Blake

Dear Friends,

How would you describe a typical Christmas at your house? Peaceful? Merry? Quality time spent with people you care about? Maybe you're not quite there, but you'd like to be.

It's easy to get caught up in the planning and shopping that so often surround the busy holiday season. In doing so, we sometimes forget what's at the true heart of the holiday: family and friends. And that's why we've created this cookbook—so you can enjoy cooking and baking yet still spend time with your family and friends.

Filled with helpful holiday hints, time-saving tips, creative menus and family fun, *Pillsbury Family Christmas Cookbook* lets you focus your time and energy on what matters most.

So start a new holiday tradition: pick a recipe or two from this book, ask your kids to lend a hand in the kitchen, dust off your Christmas videos and spend the night at home enjoying the company of family and friends. Those six boxes of Christmas decorations in the basement? They can wait.

Warmly,
The Pillsbury Editors

Contents

Introduction Create a Magical, Merry Christmas 9

1 Seasonal Starters and Snacks 16
   Tasty tidbits to jump-start your party

2 Holiday Bread Basket 44
   Sweet and savory breads for special occasions

3 Casual Get-Together Meals 70
   Easy entrées for family and friends

4 Christmas Day Entrées 106
   Extra-special recipes for the big day

5 All the Trimmings 138
   Festive side dishes and salads

6 Delectable Desserts 164
   Top off your holiday meal with a sweet treat

7 Sweet Shoppe 198
   Candies and cookies to celebrate the season

8 Homemade Gifts from the Kitchen 226
   Creative ideas to please everyone on your list

9 Kids' Workshop 244
   Fun projects to make, give and enjoy

   Helpful Nutrition and Cooking Information 262
   Index 264

INTRODUCTION

Create a Magical, Merry Christmas

When you think back upon your favorite Christmas memories, what are the first thoughts that come to mind? Waking up early on Christmas morning to a gloriously decorated tree? A beloved gift? A mouthwatering meal? Singing carols door-to-door with your siblings? Chances are that many—if not all—of your fondest moments involve someone near and dear to you: your parents or grandparents, siblings, a special aunt or uncle, your own children, a close friend or maybe even all of the above. And that's what the holidays are all about: connecting with family and friends.

Pillsbury Family Christmas Cookbook was created with that in mind. Because connecting with family and friends often involves *feeding* family and friends, recipes were selected to please a variety of palates, including picky ones, and many can serve a large number of people.

To help ensure your holiday is a happy one, you'll also find suggestions for managing seasonal stress, tips on organizing and planning holiday baking, buffet ideas and ways to involve your kids in the kitchen (without losing your mind).

'Tis the season for making even more memorable moments and, with the timely tips and delicious holiday recipes that follow, *Pillsbury Family Christmas Cookbook* is here to help!

Have a Family-Filled Happy Holiday

Christmas should come as no surprise—after all, it falls on the same date every year. And yet, year after year, it sneaks up when we're not looking. Before you know it, you have endless gifts to buy, extravagant meals to make and a house you've decided absolutely *must* look like it came from the pages of a magazine. Stop. Take a break and read the following. Although no one can make this busy season completely stress free, here are a few hints to help take some of the hassle out of your holidays.

1. Get By with a Little Help from Your Friends (and Family)

Whatever you're hosting—a Christmas cocktail party, dinner, breakfast or brunch—accept help when it's offered. When you let a friend or family member bring an appetizer, refill drinks or clear the table, you not only lighten your load, but you also help people feel good about themselves. And if no one offers, there's nothing wrong with flat out asking for help. Suggest family members or friends bring a dish you know is their specialty—something they're proud of and can't wait to share.

2. Don't Shop 'Til You Drop

You may not be able to completely avoid the hustle and bustle of your local shopping mall, but you *can* minimize the time you spend there. First, try to pare down your gift list before you even hit the malls. If you have a big family, draw names, or give one gift the whole family can enjoy instead of individual presents. Once you've compiled your list, try to come up with ideas for each person before you even leave the house. You can ease the stress of trying to find the "perfect" present by asking friends and family to create holiday wish lists. To eliminate any guesswork, be sure to ask for specifics—colors, clothes sizes and even stores where you can find the items. Or shop catalogs and the Web for presents, and have the items shipped directly to the recipients. If you can do any of the above several months ahead of the holiday, even better.

3. Just Say No

You can't be all things to all people, and the sooner you accept this fact, chances are the happier you'll be. It's not necessary to attend every holiday party or to buy gifts for everyone in your office. Baking every family member's favorite cookie is a nice thought, but it defeats the purpose if you're running yourself ragged. There's no rule requiring you to bring a homemade potluck dish to every holiday gathering. A bottle of wine, a store-bought meat and cheese platter or a simple deli salad are all completely acceptable potluck fare.

4. Focus on Family

Try not to forget what the season is really about: love and friendship, family and friends. In addition to all those boxes under the tree, your time is also a gift. Your children are more likely to remember a special night spent together as a family than a gift they'll tire of down the road. Taking a night off is not "doing nothing"; it's allowing yourself to focus on what really matters and enjoy the company of those around you. If you can't make it home for the holidays, create your own family by inviting others who also aren't able to go home.

5. Count Your Blessings

Perhaps your tree doesn't look exactly how you want it to, or maybe you weren't able to track down that hard-to-find toy your son is begging for, but all is not lost. If you're surrounded by family and friends, you're better off than a lot of people. Should you find yourself getting caught up in the chaos that so often is Christmas, try volunteering at a soup kitchen or buying a gift for someone who is less fortunate to give you a fresh perspective.

6. Great Expectations

It's great to strive for perfection, but if you find yourself feeling frustrated again and again, perhaps you need to rethink your standards. You may find that doing less and spending more time with family and friends will leave you feeling far more satisfied. Perfect families, gifts and houses exist only on TV and in the movies. Although it's wonderful to aim to be and do your best, sometimes your time is better spent accepting the way things are.

Start Your Ovens: Holiday Baking 101

It's never too early to start organizing and planning for the busy baking season. To help avoid Christmas crises, keep the following tips in mind.

❄ Stock up on staples. Before the holiday rush starts, buy big bags of flour and sugar and extra baking powder, extracts and flavorings. Refrigerated cookie dough, pie crusts and crescent rolls and frozen biscuits and dinner rolls are all great to have on hand during the holidays. Watch your local paper for bargains and coupons.

❄ Bake ahead. Decide which cookies, cakes, pies, breads and other baked goods and candies you could make ahead (for recipe ideas, see Holiday Head Start, page 14). Then bake goods in disposable foil pans for easy gift-giving.

❄ Host a candy exchange. Invite eight to twelve friends to bring one dozen of their favorite candies or sweets, and divide them all among you. Provide hot chocolate or store-bought eggnog to drink, and you'll have an instant party.

❄ Hold a holiday bake fest. Set aside a whole day just for baking (for recipe ideas, see Holiday Head Start, page 14). Double the fun by asking a relative or friend to join you. Provide the basics, such as flour, eggs and sugar, and ask the other person to bring any special ingredients they may need for their recipes. Put on some classic Christmas music to get you in the holiday spirit. At the end of the day, divide the goodies between you. It's a great way to get your baking done and catch up with what's happening with your family or friends at the same time.

❄ Let the kids lend a hand. Buy a bunch of refrigerated dough and bake the cookies ahead of time. Then let your kids invite several friends over to decorate them. Just turn them loose with the frosting and sugar sprinkles.

❄ Make double batches. Keep one for yourself; give the other as gifts.

Holiday Buffet Tips & Tricks

Hosting a buffet is a wonderful way to entertain during the holiday. It's casual, requires less dining space and tends to create a more relaxed atmosphere than a sit-down dinner. It also allows you to mix and mingle with your guests easily because you don't have to spend nearly as much time in the kitchen. Here are some helpful hints for making your holiday buffet a smashing success.

❋ A buffet doesn't have to be a whole meal. Consider having a dessert or appetizer buffet or a pasta or potato bar. A coffee bar is a hip and fun idea when served with an assortment of accompaniments, such as brandy, rum, whiskey and coffee liqueur.

❋ Let the number of guests decide where you put your buffet table. More guests require more elbow room, so your best bet is to station the table in a spot where people can access both sides.

❋ A stack of plates usually marks the spot where the buffet starts. Provide napkins and silverware at the end of the table. That way, your guests can easily pick them up once their plates are filled. Unless you plan to provide small sit-down tables for everyone, it's best to stick with forks; knives are difficult to use when standing up (this is also good to keep in mind when choosing what food to serve as well). The same idea applies to serving utensils: salad tongs are easier to handle with one hand than a salad fork and spoon.

❋ Pick foods that are easy to serve (see above) and that stand up well over time. Slow cooker items are good choices, as are casseroles and tossed and molded salads. Include entrées that vary in serving temps and cooking methods, and try to make as many make-ahead dishes as you can (for recipe ideas, see Holiday Head Start, page 14).

❋ To keep traffic jams to a minimum, you may want to set up separate buffets, one for savory items and another for desserts and sweets.

❋ The buffet table is the center of interest so you'll want to decorate it with care. Formal or informal? It's up to you. A linen tablecloth, festive place mats and beautiful serving trays are just a few ways to dress up the table. For more table decorations, see pages 51, 77, 129, 150 and 249.

Holiday Head Start

Many appetizers and desserts in this cookbook can be made ahead, freeing you up for other last-minute details. Here are just a few of the make-ahead choices:

Creole Meatballs, page 21
Beef Tenderloin and Caramelized Onion Sandwiches, page 22
Cilantro-Lime Shrimp with Chile Aïoli, page 35
Fried Ravioli with Tomato Sauce, page 37
Nutty Holiday Popcorn, page 43
Chocolate-Almond Mousse Cake, page 166
Christmas Angel Cake, page 168
Dark Gingerbread Bundt Cake, page 172
Strawberry-Fudge Pie, page 177
Orange Crème Dessert with Ruby Cranberry Sauce, page 182
Chocolate-Cherry Cheesecake, page 187
Spiced Cider Cheesecake, page 188
Mocha Truffle Cheesecake, page 190
Cranberry-Peach Gingerbread Trifle, page 192
Eggnog Bread Pudding with Cherry-Bourbon Sauce, page 193
Creamy Peppermint-Topped Brownie Dessert, page 195
Caffé Latte Crème Brûlée, page 196
Cranberry Mousse, page 197
Cardamom Sandwich Cookies, page 205
Mint Kissed Meringues, page 210
Spiced Walnut Brittle, page 218
Cranberry-Walnut White Fudge, page 219
Holiday Spiced Nuts, page 242
Snowman Faces, page 254
Sugar Cone Trees, page 256

Kids in the Kitchen

You may be tempted to scoot the kids out of the kitchen when you do your holiday baking, but involving them in the process is actually a great way to create magical, memorable moments. To help ensure a happy, tears-free experience for everyone, keep the following in mind:

1. Cooking can get messy, so have kids cover up with an apron or an old shirt with the sleeves rolled up. Children with longer hair may want to pull it back so it doesn't get in the way (and in the food).
2. Ask kids to wash their hands before you begin baking. Remind them to rewash after sneezing or using the bathroom.
3. Read over the recipe with the children so that everyone knows what is needed and what needs to be done. Ask if anyone has any questions before you begin.
4. Organize the project by yourself ahead of time, or have the kids help you gather utensils and ingredients. Either way, make sure you have everything you need before you start so you can avoid having a bunch of squirming kids as you search for stuff.
5. Have damp cloths and sponges available so kids can clean up as they go. A drop cloth spread underneath the work area helps keep food fallout to a minimum. To make final cleanup easier, have the kids put dirty dishes in a sink of soapy water as they work.
6. Be kind to the earth. Ask kids to put cans and foil, bottles and glass and plastic containers in their proper recycling spots.
7. Start a keepsake recipe box to keep track of favorite recipes. Make notes about what you'd do differently next time.

1 Seasonal Starters and Snacks

Beef Crostini with Caper Mayonnaise 18

Pastrami and Pepper Roll-ups 19

Chili Cheese Dip and Potato Wedges 20

Creole Meatballs 21

Beef Tenderloin and Caramelized Onion
Sandwiches 22

Pork Tenderloin Crostini 24

Saucy Sausage Medallions 26

Turkey-Cranberry Quesadillas 27

Chicken Peanut Kabobs 29

Teriyaki Seafood-Stuffed Mushrooms 30

Asian Crab Mini Quiches 32

Smoked Salmon on Endive 33

Cilantro-Lime Shrimp
with Chile Aïoli 35

Fried Ravioli with Tomato Sauce 37

Mini Pizzas 38

Cherry-Cheese Spread 40

Goat Cheese and Olive Phyllo Purses 42

Nutty Holiday Popcorn 43

beef crostini with caper mayonnaise

Prep Time: 30 minutes

24 (¼- to ½-inch-thick) slices baguette or small French bread

2 tablespoons olive oil

½ cup mayonnaise

¼ cup grated Parmesan cheese

2 tablespoons chopped fresh chives

2 to 4 tablespoons drained capers

¼ teaspoon garlic powder

½ lb. thinly sliced cooked roast beef (from deli), cut into 24 pieces

2 Italian plum tomatoes, cut into 24 thin slices

Chopped fresh chives, if desired

1. Heat oven to 350°F. Place bread slices on ungreased cookie sheet; brush lightly with oil. Bake at 350°F. for 8 to 10 minutes or until crisp. Cool 5 minutes or until completely cooled.

2. Meanwhile, in small bowl, combine mayonnaise, cheese, 2 tablespoons chives, the capers and garlic powder; mix well.

3. Spread about ½ tablespoon mayonnaise mixture on each toasted bread slice. Top each with 1 piece of roast beef and 1 slice of tomato. Garnish with chives.

Yield: 24 appetizers

NUTRITION INFORMATION PER SERVING
Serving Size: 1 Appetizer; Calories 80; Calories from Fat 55 **% Daily Value:** Total Fat 6g 9%; Saturated Fat 1g 5%; Cholesterol 10mg 3%; Sodium 190mg 8%; Total Carbohydrate 3g 1%; Dietary Fiber 0g 0%; Sugars 0g; Protein 3g; Vitamin A 0%; Vitamin C 0%; Calcium 2%; Iron 2% **Dietary Exchanges:** ½ Medium-Fat Meat, 1 Fat, 0 Carbohydrate Choice

Special Touch

Love the taste of garlic? Chop a clove of garlic and heat with the olive oil in the microwave for about 20 seconds before brushing it onto the bread.

pastrami and pepper roll-ups

Prep Time: 25 minutes   (Ready in 2 hours 25 minutes)

½ lb. thinly sliced pastrami (from deli)

⅓ cup chive and onion cream cheese spread (from 8-oz. container)

½ cup roasted red bell peppers (from a jar), drained, cut into ¾-inch-wide strips

Fresh rosemary sprigs, if desired

1. Spread each pastrami slice with cream cheese spread. Top each with roasted pepper piece at one edge. Starting at roasted pepper edge, roll up each tightly. Cover; refrigerate at least 2 hours or until firm.

2. To serve, cut each roll into 1-inch-thick pieces. Secure each with fresh rosemary sprig or cocktail toothpick.

Yield: 40 appetizers

NUTRITION INFORMATION PER SERVING
Serving Size: 1 Appetizer; Calories 15; Calories from Fat 10 **% Daily Value:** Total Fat 1g 2%; Saturated Fat 1g 5%; Cholesterol 5mg 2%; Sodium 80mg 3%; Total Carbohydrate 0g 0%; Dietary Fiber 0g 0%; Sugars 0g; Protein 1g; Vitamin A 2%; Vitamin C 4%; Calcium 0%; Iron 0% **Dietary Exchanges:** Free, 0 Carbohydrate Choice

Family Ties

Involve the whole family when making this appetizer. One person can spread the cream cheese, another can top with the roasted peppers and a third can be in charge of rolling up the appetizers. Getting ready for a party has never been so much fun!

chili cheese dip
and potato wedges

Prep Time: 25 minutes

1 (24-oz.) pkg. frozen potato wedges with skins

½ lb. lean ground beef

1 small onion, chopped (about ⅓ cup)

8 oz. pasteurized prepared cheese product, cut into chunks (2 cups)

1 (8-oz.) can tomato sauce

1 (4.5-oz.) can chopped green chiles, drained

1. Heat oven to 450°F. Bake potato wedges as directed on package.

2. Meanwhile, in large saucepan, cook ground beef and onion over medium-high heat for 5 to 7 minutes or until beef is thoroughly cooked, stirring frequently. Drain. Add cheese, tomato sauce and chiles; mix well. Cook over low heat until cheese is melted and mixture is hot, stirring frequently.

3. Serve hot potato wedges with cheese dip.

Yield: 24 servings

NUTRITION INFORMATION PER SERVING
Serving Size: ¹⁄₂₄ of Recipe; Calories 115; Calories from Fat 55 **% Daily Value:** Total Fat 6g 9%; Saturated Fat 2g 10%; Cholesterol 15mg 5%; Sodium 300mg 13%; Total Carbohydrate 11g 4%; Dietary Fiber 1g 4%; Sugars 2g; Protein 4g; Vitamin A 4%; Vitamin C 4%; Calcium 4%; Iron 2% **Dietary Exchanges:** 1 Starch, 1 Fat, 1 Carbohydrate Choice

creole meatballs

Prep Time: 50 minutes

1 egg

1½ lb. lean ground beef

½ cup Italian-style dry bread crumbs

¼ cup chopped onion

¼ cup chopped green bell pepper

¾ teaspoon salt

½ teaspoon celery salt

¼ teaspoon ground red pepper (cayenne)

1 (15-oz.) can tomato sauce

2 tablespoons vegetable oil

2 tablespoons all-purpose flour

2 tablespoons currant jelly

1 teaspoon Worcestershire sauce

½ teaspoon dried Italian seasoning

¼ teaspoon garlic salt

1. Heat oven to 400°F. Beat egg in large bowl. Add ground beef, bread crumbs, onion, bell pepper, salt, celery salt, ⅛ teaspoon of the ground red pepper and 2 tablespoons of the tomato sauce; mix well. Shape mixture into 48 (1¼-inch) meatballs, using about 1 tablespoon mixture for each. Place in ungreased 15×10×1-inch baking pan.

2. Bake at 400°F. for 15 to 20 minutes or until thoroughly cooked and no longer pink in center.

3. Meanwhile, heat oil in medium saucepan over medium-high heat until hot. With wire whisk, stir in flour; cook and stir until mixture turns a deep, rich brown color. Stir in remaining ⅛ teaspoon ground red pepper, remaining tomato sauce and all remaining ingredients. Bring to a boil. Cook an additional minute, stirring constantly.

4. Add cooked meatballs to sauce; stir gently to coat. Serve with cocktail toothpicks.

Yield: 48 meatballs

NUTRITION INFORMATION PER SERVING
Serving Size: 1 Meatball; Calories 45; Calories from Fat 25 % **Daily Value:** Total Fat 3g 5%; Saturated Fat 1g 5%; Cholesterol 10mg 3%; Sodium 130mg 5%; Total Carbohydrate 2g 1%; Dietary Fiber 0g 0%; Sugars 1g; Protein 3g; Vitamin A 2%; Vitamin C 0%; Calcium 0%; Iron 2% **Dietary Exchanges:** ½ Medium-Fat Meat, 0 Carbohydrate Choice

Do-Ahead

To make these spicy meatballs a day ahead, prepare the recipe as directed and transfer the meatballs and sauce to a baking dish. Cool, cover and refrigerate. To serve, heat dish in a 350°F. oven, or transfer the meatballs and sauce to a saucepan and heat gently over low heat until hot. Either method takes about 10 minutes.

beef tenderloin and caramelized onion sandwiches

Prep Time: 45 minutes   (Ready in 1 hour 30 minutes)

1 teaspoon salt

¼ teaspoon garlic powder

¼ teaspoon paprika

¼ teaspoon coarse ground black pepper

1 (1-lb.) beef tenderloin, trimmed

3 tablespoons butter

1 tablespoon vegetable oil

2 tablespoons brown sugar

3 medium onions, cut into ¼-inch-thick slices

2 tablespoons dry red wine or water

½ cup sour cream

1 tablespoon purchased horseradish sauce

1 (10-inch) round loaf focaccia (Italian flat bread)

1½ cups firmly packed baby spinach leaves

Cocktail toothpicks

1. Heat oven to 450°F. In small bowl, combine ½ teaspoon of the salt, the garlic powder, paprika and pepper; mix well. Rub mixture on all surfaces of beef tenderloin. Place beef in small shallow roasting pan; tuck thin end under.

2. Bake at 450°F. for 20 to 25 minutes or until meat thermometer inserted in center registers 140°F. for rare. Cool 30 minutes or until completely cooled; slice very thin.

3. Meanwhile, in large skillet, heat butter and oil over medium heat until butter melts. Add brown sugar and onions; stir to coat. Cook over medium heat for 10 minutes or until onions begin to soften, stirring occasionally. Add wine. Reduce heat to medium-low; cover and cook 10 to 15 minutes or until onions are very tender.

4. Combine sour cream, horseradish sauce and remaining ½ teaspoon salt; mix well. Heat focaccia as directed on package; cut in half horizontally. Spread both cut sides with sour cream mixture. Arrange spinach leaves on bottom half of focaccia; top with beef slices. Top with onions and top half of focaccia; press down.

5. Insert toothpicks through all layers at 1¼- to 1½-inch intervals. Cut between toothpicks to form tiny sandwich squares.

Yield: 36 sandwiches

NUTRITION INFORMATION PER SERVING
Serving Size: 1 Sandwich; Calories 80; Calories from Fat 35 % **Daily Value:** Total Fat 4g 6%; Saturated Fat 2g 10%; Cholesterol 10mg 3%; Sodium 170mg 7%; Total Carbohydrate 7g 2%; Dietary Fiber 0g 0%; Sugars 1g; Protein 4g; Vitamin A 4%; Vitamin C 0%; Calcium 0%; Iron 4% **Dietary Exchanges:** ½ Starch, ½ Lean Meat, ½ Fat, ½ Carbohydrate Choice

Do-Ahead
Bake the beef tenderloin and cook the onions as directed. Wrap the tenderloin and place the onions in a covered container, and refrigerate up to 24 hours. Just before serving, prepare the sauce and assemble sandwiches as directed in recipe.

individual candle place setting

1. Spray a 3-inch grapevine wreath with gold metallic spray paint; let dry.

2. Attach jingle bells, flat-sided gold stones, buttons and bulbs to wreath with craft wire or glue.

3. Place wreath on plate or small candle stand. Place candle in wreath.

pork tenderloin crostini

Prep Time: 50 minutes   (Ready in 2 hours 20 minutes)

3 green onions

1 (0.9-oz.) pkg. béarnaise sauce mix

¾ cup milk

¼ cup butter

1 lb. (2 small) pork tenderloins

1 teaspoon garlic salt

¼ teaspoon coarsely ground black pepper

32 thin slices baguette-style French bread

4 teaspoons crushed pink peppercorns or finely chopped red bell pepper

1. Chop onions, separating white portion from green. Place white portion in small saucepan; reserve green portion. Add sauce mix and milk to saucepan; beat with wire whisk to combine. Add butter; cook over medium heat until mixture comes to a boil, stirring constantly. Reduce heat to low; simmer 1 minute. Cover; refrigerate at least 2 hours or until thickened and cool.

2. Meanwhile, heat oven to 400°F. Place pork tenderloins in shallow roasting pan; rub surfaces with garlic salt and pepper. Bake at 400°F. for 25 to 30 minutes or until no longer pink in center and meat thermometer inserted in center registers 160°F. Cool 20 minutes or until cool enough to handle and slice.

3. Reduce oven temperature to 375°F. Place bread slices on ungreased cookie sheet. Bake at 375°F. for 7 to 9 minutes or until crisp. Cool 10 minutes or until completely cooled.

4. To serve, stir reserved green portion of onions into sauce. Cut pork into 32 slices. Place 1 slice pork on each toasted bread slice, folding pork if necessary. Top each with 1 teaspoon sauce; reserve remainder for another use. Top each with ⅛ teaspoon crushed pink peppercorns.

Yield: 32 appetizers

NUTRITION INFORMATION PER SERVING
Serving Size: 1 Appetizer; Calories 60; Calories from Fat 20 % **Daily Value:** Total Fat 2g 3%; Saturated Fat 1g 5%; Cholesterol 15mg 5%; Sodium 110mg 5%; Total Carbohydrate 6g 2%; Dietary Fiber 0g 0%; Sugars 0g; Protein 4g; Vitamin A 2%; Vitamin C 0%; Calcium 2%; Iron 2% **Dietary Exchanges:** ½ Starch, ½ Lean Meat, ½ Carbohydrate Choice

Family Ties

To make sure no one goes home hungry, you may want to have some tiny pork sandwiches on hand to please youngsters who may not care for the béarnaise sauce and the pink peppercorns.

saucy sausage medallions

Prep Time: 30 minutes

1 tablespoon olive oil

¼ cup finely chopped onion

3 garlic cloves, minced

1 lb. cooked Polish sausage or kielbasa links, cut into ½-inch-thick slices

1 teaspoon paprika

½ teaspoon coriander

Dash ground red pepper (cayenne)

1 (8-oz.) can tomato sauce

¼ cup dry red wine or water

1. Heat oil in large skillet over medium heat until hot. Add onion; cook 4 to 5 minutes or until softened, stirring occasionally.

2. Add garlic; cook and stir 30 to 60 seconds or until fragrant. Add sausage slices; cook 2 to 4 minutes or until lightly browned, turning once.

3. Stir in paprika, coriander and ground red pepper. Add tomato sauce and wine; mix well. Cook about 5 minutes to reduce liquid slightly, stirring occasionally. Serve with cocktail toothpicks.

Yield: 20 servings

Substitution

Spanish smoked chorizo is another linked sausage that's right on the money when it comes to making these tasty coins. Use it in place of the Polish sausage or kielbasa links.

turkey-cranberry quesadillas

Prep Time: 25 minutes

8 (6- to 7-inch) flour tortillas

1 (10- or 12-oz.) container cranberry-orange sauce, thawed if frozen

6 oz. thinly sliced smoked turkey

5 oz. Havarti cheese, thinly sliced

1 tablespoon oil

1. Top each of 4 tortillas with 1 tablespoon of the cranberry-orange sauce; spread to edges. Top each with turkey, cheese and second tortilla.

2. Heat medium skillet over medium heat until hot. Brush 1 side of 1 quesadilla with oil. Place oiled side down in skillet; press down with pancake turner. Cook 1 to 2 minutes or until browned.

3. Brush top of quesadilla with oil. Flip quesadilla; cook an additional 1 to 2 minutes or until browned and cheese is melted. Repeat with remaining quesadillas.

4. To serve, cut each quesadilla into 6 wedges. Serve quesadillas with remaining cranberry-orange sauce.

Yield: 24 servings

NUTRITION INFORMATION PER SERVING
Serving Size: 1 Quesadilla; Calories 90; Calories from Fat 35 **% Daily Value:** Total Fat 4g 6%; Saturated Fat 2g 10%; Cholesterol 10mg 3%; Sodium 170mg 7%; Total Carbohydrate 10g 3%; Dietary Fiber 0g 0%; Sugars 5g; Protein 3g; Vitamin A 2%; Vitamin C 2%; Calcium 4%; Iron 2% **Dietary Exchanges:** ½ Starch, 1 Fat, ½ Carbohydrate Choice

Family Ties
Kids and dipping food go hand in hand. Up the fun factor by letting kids dunk their own quesadillas in the cranberry-orange sauce. Who knew hors d'oeuvres could be such a blast?

chicken peanut kabobs

Prep Time: 30 minutes

kabob

20 (6-inch) bamboo or wooden skewers

10 slices bacon

4 boneless skinless chicken breast halves

sauce

¼ cup peanut butter

¼ cup soy sauce

¼ cup apple juice or water

¼ to ½ teaspoon crushed red pepper flakes

1. Soak skewers in water for 15 minutes. Meanwhile, cut each bacon slice into 4 pieces, then cook in large nonstick skillet over medium heat for about 5 minutes or until partially cooked but not crisp. Remove bacon from skillet; drain on paper towels.

2. Cut each chicken breast half lengthwise into 5 strips, each about ½ inch thick. Cut each strip into 3 pieces. Alternately thread 3 chicken pieces and 2 cooked bacon pieces onto each skewer; place on broiler pan.

3. In small bowl, combine all sauce ingredients; mix well. Pour half of sauce into small serving bowl, and set aside until serving time.

4. Brush about half of reserved sauce evenly over kabobs. Broil kabobs 4 to 6 inches from heat for 3 to 4 minutes. Brush remaining sauce over kabobs; turn kabobs. Broil an additional 3 to 4 minutes or until chicken is no longer pink in center. Serve with reserved sauce.

Yield: 20 kabobs

NUTRITION INFORMATION PER SERVING
Serving Size: 1 Kabob; Calories 60; Calories from Fat 25 **% Daily Value:** Total Fat 3g 5%; Saturated Fat 1g 5%; Cholesterol 15mg 5%; Sodium 160mg 7%; Total Carbohydrate 1g 1%; Dietary Fiber 0g 0%; Sugars 0g; Protein 7g; Vitamin A 0%; Vitamin C 0%; Calcium 0%; Iron 2% **Dietary Exchanges:** 1 Very Lean Meat, ½ Fat, 0 Carbohydrate Choice

Do-Ahead

Nutty entertaining schedule? Save time by threading the bamboo skewers with the bacon-topped chicken prior to party time. Cover and refrigerate the skewers for up to four hours. Brush the skewers with peanut sauce and broil them just before you're ready to serve.

teriyaki seafood-stuffed mushrooms

Prep Time: 45 minutes   (Ready in 1 hour 15 minutes)

48 (1½- to 2-inch) fresh whole mushrooms, washed

2 garlic cloves, minced

2¼ cups water

1 (10-oz.) bottle teriyaki sauce

⅓ cup chopped imitation crabmeat (surimi)

⅓ cup chopped water chestnuts

1 tablespoon chopped fresh chives

1. Remove stems from mushrooms; discard or reserve for a future use.

2. In Dutch oven, combine mushroom caps, garlic, water and teriyaki sauce. Bring to a boil over medium-high heat. Reduce heat to low; cover and simmer 15 to 20 minutes or until mushrooms are thoroughly cooked, stirring occasionally.

3. Drain mushrooms; place on paper towels to dry. Cool about 15 minutes or until completely cooled.

4. Meanwhile, in medium bowl, combine imitation crabmeat and water chestnuts; mix well.

5. Fill each mushroom cap with about ½ teaspoon crabmeat mixture. Sprinkle each with chives. Serve immediately, or cover and refrigerate until serving time.

Yield: *48 appetizers*

Substitution

It's easy to make these stuffed mushrooms vegetarian—just replace the surimi with bell peppers. Play up the holiday theme by using red and green bell peppers. To keep the colors fresh, finely chop the peppers and combine them with the water chestnuts just before serving.

asian crab mini quiches

Prep Time: 20 minutes   (Ready in 50 minutes)

1 (15-oz.) pkg. refrigerated pie crusts, softened as directed on package

2 eggs

½ cup half-and-half

2 tablespoons chopped green onions

1 red jalapeño chile, seeded, minced (about 2 tablespoons)

1 teaspoon grated lime peel

1 teaspoon grated gingerroot

½ teaspoon salt

1 (6-oz.) can refrigerated pasteurized crabmeat

1 oz. (¼ cup) shredded fresh Parmesan cheese

1. Heat oven to 375°F. Remove pie crusts from pouches. Unfold crusts; press out fold lines. With 2½-inch round cutter, cut crusts into 24 rounds. Press each round into ungreased miniature muffin cup.

2. Beat eggs in medium bowl. Add half-and-half, onions, chile, lime peel, gingerroot and salt; beat with wire whisk until well blended. Stir in crabmeat and cheese. Spoon about 1 tablespoon mixture into each crust-lined cup.

3. Bake at 375°F. for 25 to 30 minutes or until filling is set and crust is golden brown around edges. Serve warm or cool. Store in refrigerator.

Yield: 24 appetizers

Family Ties
Cutting the pie crust into rounds is kind of like cutting cookie dough. Why not let the kids help out? If you don't have enough cutters, a drinking glass with a similar size mouth will work, too.

smoked salmon on endive

Prep Time: 25 minutes

1 (8-oz.) container chive and onion cream cheese spread

1 (4.5-oz.) pkg. smoked salmon, skin removed, finely chopped

2 tablespoons mayonnaise

1/8 teaspoon hot pepper sauce

24 leaves Belgian endive (2 to 3 heads)

Chopped fresh chives, if desired

1. In medium bowl, combine all ingredients except endive and chives; mix well. Spoon or pipe scant tablespoon mixture into each endive leaf.

2. Serve immediately, or cover and refrigerate until serving time. Just before serving, sprinkle with chives.

Yield: 24 appetizers

Special Touch

A large open star tip works well if piping the cheese mixture onto the Belgian endive leaves. The star tip adds an artistic touch and works better than a small tip, which will become clogged with the bits of salmon in the cheese mixture.

NUTRITION INFORMATION PER SERVING
Serving Size: 1 Appetizer; Calories 50; Calories from Fat 35 **% Daily Value:** Total Fat 4g 6%; Saturated Fat 2g 10%; Cholesterol 10mg 3%; Sodium 80mg 3%; Total Carbohydrate 1g 1%; Dietary Fiber 0g 0%; Sugars 0g; Protein 2g; Vitamin A 6%; Vitamin C 0%; Calcium 0%; Iron 0% **Dietary Exchanges:** 1/2 Lean Meat, 1/2 Fat, 0 Carbohydrate Choice

cilantro-lime shrimp
with chile aïoli

Prep Time: 30 minutes

shrimp

24 fresh uncooked large shrimp (about 1 lb.), shelled with tails left on

1 tablespoon chopped fresh cilantro

2 tablespoons lime juice

1 tablespoon olive oil

1 garlic clove, minced

chile aïoli

1 cup mayonnaise

3 tablespoons milk

2 canned chipotle chiles in adobo sauce, chopped (about 4 teaspoons)

2 garlic cloves, chopped

2 teaspoons chopped fresh cilantro

1. Heat oven to 350°F. Cut shrimp along outside curve almost to other side; spread open. Remove any visible vein. Place cut side down on ungreased cookie sheet so that tails curve up.

2. In small bowl, combine all remaining shrimp ingredients; mix well. Brush mixture over shrimp.

3. Bake at 350°F. for 5 to 7 minutes or until shrimp turn pink.

4. Meanwhile, in blender container, combine all chile aïoli ingredients except cilantro; blend until smooth.

5. To serve, drizzle small amount of aïoli onto serving platter. Sprinkle with 2 teaspoons chopped cilantro. Place cooked shrimp over aïoli. Serve with remaining aïoli.

Yield: 24 servings

NUTRITION INFORMATION PER SERVING
Serving Size: ¹⁄₂₄ of Recipe; Calories 80; Calories from Fat 70 **% Daily Value:** Total Fat 8g 12%; Saturated Fat 1g 5%; Cholesterol 15mg 5%; Sodium 70mg 3%; Total Carbohydrate 1g 1%; Dietary Fiber 0g 0%; Sugars 0g; Protein 1g; Vitamin A 0%; Vitamin C 0%; Calcium 0%; Iron 0% **Dietary Exchanges:** 1½ Fat, 0 Carbohydrate Choice

Do-Ahead
This delicious dish can be made up to four hours ahead of time. Prepare the shrimp, lime juice mixture and chile aïoli ahead. Cover and refrigerate. Just before serving, brush the lime juice mixture on the shrimp, then broil. Serve the shrimp with the chile aïoli as directed.

a touch of glass

1. Add sugar crystals or fresh cranberries to a shallow glass bowl.

2. Arrange a candle, greenery, ornaments and ribbon in the sugar.

fried ravioli with tomato sauce

Prep Time: 45 minutes

1 (15-oz.) can tomato sauce

1 cup finely chopped fresh tomato (about 1 large)

½ cup finely chopped sun-dried tomatoes packed in olive oil and herbs

1 teaspoon dried Italian seasoning

1 quart (4 cups) vegetable oil for deep-frying

1 (25-oz.) pkg. frozen small square cheese-filled ravioli, thawed, or 1 (20-oz.) pkg. refrigerated 4-cheese ravioli, thawed

2 tablespoons chopped green onion tops

1. In medium saucepan, combine tomato sauce, fresh tomato, sun-dried tomatoes and Italian seasoning; mix well. Bring to a boil. Reduce heat to medium-low; simmer 15 to 20 minutes or until thickened, stirring occasionally.

2. Meanwhile, heat oil in large heavy saucepan over medium-high heat to 375°F. Pat ravioli dry with paper towels. Fry ravioli, about 6 at a time, for 1 to 3 minutes or until golden and crisp, turning once. Drain on paper towels.

3. Pour sauce into serving bowl; sprinkle with onions. Serve warm ravioli with warm dipping sauce.

Yield: 40 servings

Do-Ahead

Get a head start on your party preparations by making this satisfying snack a day ahead. Prepare the ravioli and the sauce and cool separately. Cover and refrigerate both for up to one day. To serve, arrange the ravioli in a single layer on a cookie sheet and reheat in a 350°F. oven for about 10 minutes or until the ravioli are hot. Reheat the sauce on the stovetop over low heat for 5 to 10 minutes or until hot.

NUTRITION INFORMATION PER SERVING
Serving Size: ¹⁄₄₀ of Recipe; Calories 50; Calories from Fat 25 **% Daily Value:** Total Fat 3g 5%; Saturated Fat 1g 5%; Cholesterol 20mg 7%; Sodium 210mg 9%; Total Carbohydrate 4g 1%; Dietary Fiber 0g 0%; Sugars 1g; Protein 2g; Vitamin A 4%; Vitamin C 2%; Calcium 4%; Iron 2% **Dietary Exchanges:** ½ Medium-Fat Meat, ½ Fat, 0 Carbohydrate Choice

mini pizzas

1 (13.8-oz.) can refrigerated pizza crust

¼ cup purchased pesto

18 slices Italian plum tomatoes

5 (1-oz.) slices mozzarella cheese, cut into 18 (1½-inch) squares

1. Heat oven to 425°F. Lightly spray cookie sheet with non-stick cooking spray. Unroll dough onto sprayed cookie sheet. Press dough with fingers to form 15×10-inch rectangle.

2. With 2½-inch holiday-shaped metal cookie cutters, cut dough into 18 shapes; remove excess dough. Bake at 425°F. for 6 to 8 minutes or until set.

3. Remove partially baked crusts from oven; cool 3 to 4 minutes. Spread each crust with pesto. Top each with 1 tomato slice and 1 cheese square.

4. Return to oven; bake an additional 3 to 5 minutes or until cheese is melted and edges are browned.

Yield: 18 mini pizzas

Family Ties

Kids will love personalizing these tiny pizzas. Let them cut out the dough with cookie cutters and then pile on pepperoni, cheese and olives as they see fit. The sky's the limit when it comes to topping these mini morsels.

NUTRITION INFORMATION PER SERVING
Serving Size: 1 Mini Pizza; Calories 85; Calories from Fat 35 **% Daily Value:** Total Fat 4g 6%; Saturated Fat 1g 5%; Cholesterol 5mg 2%; Sodium 190mg 8%; Total Carbohydrate 8g 3%; Dietary Fiber 0g 0%; Sugars 1g; Protein 4g; Vitamin A 2%; Vitamin C 0%; Calcium 6%; Iron 2% **Dietary Exchanges:** ½ Starch, ½ Medium-Fat Meat, ½ Carbohydrate Choice

holiday packages

1. Place a food gift in a small basket.

2. Add other items as appropriate. (Pair a
   muffin mix with a muffin tin and a
   decorative hot pad, as an example.)

3. Wrap the basket with colored cellophane,
   and tie with a bow or a twist of silver or gold
   star garland.

cherry-cheese spread

Prep Time: 15 minutes   (Ready in 25 hours 15 minutes)

1 (8-oz.) pkg. cream cheese, cubed

4 oz. Havarti cheese, cubed

4 oz. smoky Swiss cheese, shredded (1 cup)

1 oz. (¼ cup) crumbled blue cheese

¼ cup slivered almonds

3 tablespoons cherry-flavored liqueur or ¼ teaspoon almond extract

1 teaspoon chopped shallot

¼ cup dried cherries, chopped

1. Let all cheeses stand at room temperature for at least 30 minutes to soften. If using a mold for the cheese spread, line mold with cheesecloth.

2. Meanwhile, heat oven to 350°F. Spread almonds on ungreased cookie sheet. Bake at 350°F. for 5 to 7 minutes or until golden brown, stirring occasionally. Cool.

3. In food processor bowl with metal blade, combine all cheeses, liqueur and shallot; process until smooth. Add cherries and almonds; process with on/off pulses until almonds are chopped. Spoon cheese spread into mold lined with cheesecloth, crock or small bowl; cover. Refrigerate at least 24 hours to blend flavors.

4. About 30 minutes before serving, unmold cheese spread onto plate; remove cheesecloth. Let spread stand at room temperature for 30 minutes to soften. Serve with thin slices of baguette-style French bread, assorted crackers, celery sticks or fresh pea pods.

Yield: 2¼ cups

NUTRITION INFORMATION PER SERVING
Serving Size: 2 Tablespoons; Calories 120; Calories from Fat 90 **% Daily Value:** Total Fat 10g 15%; Saturated Fat 6g 30%; Cholesterol 30mg 10%; Sodium 120mg 5%; Total Carbohydrate 3g 1%; Dietary Fiber 0g 0%; Sugars 2g; Protein 5g; Vitamin A 6%; Vitamin C 0%; Calcium 12%; Iron 0% **Dietary Exchanges:** ½ High-Fat Meat, 1½ Fat, 0 Carbohydrate Choice

Substitution
Crazy for cranberries? Go ahead and use them instead of the dried cherries. Or try substituting golden raisins for the cherries.

goat cheese and olive phyllo purses

Prep Time: 45 minutes

6 (17×12-inch) sheets frozen phyllo (filo) pastry, thawed

¼ cup butter, melted

2 (3.5- to 4-oz.) logs chèvre (goat cheese), cut into 12 pieces

12 pitted kalamata olives, drained, patted dry and each cut in half

1. Heat oven to 400°F. Place 1 sheet of phyllo pastry on cutting board. (Cover remaining sheets with slightly damp towel.) Brush sheet with melted butter. Cut sheet in half lengthwise; cut each half into 4 equal pieces. Stack 4 pieces on top of one another, offsetting corners each time to fan. Repeat with other 4 pieces.

2. Place 1 piece of chèvre in center of each stack. Top each with 2 olive halves. Gather and pleat pastry around cheese to form "purse"; place on ungreased cookie sheet. Repeat with remaining sheets of phyllo pastry, cheese and olives.

3. Bake at 400°F for 12 to 14 minutes or until deep golden brown and crisp. Immediately remove from cookie sheet; place on wire rack. Cool 5 minutes before serving.

Yield: 12 appetizers

NUTRITION INFORMATION PER SERVING
Serving Size: 1 Appetizer; Calories 135; Calories from Fat 80 **% Daily Value:** Total Fat 9g 14%; Saturated Fat 6g 30%; Cholesterol 25mg 8%; Sodium 190mg 8%; Total Carbohydrate 8g 3%; Dietary Fiber 0g 0%; Sugars 1g; Protein 5g; Vitamin A 8%; Vitamin C 0%; Calcium 6%; Iron 4% **Dietary Exchanges:** ½ Starch, ½ High-Fat Meat, 1 Fat, ½ Carbohydrate Choice

Special Touch
To make these "purses" look more like holiday presents, tie the green portion of a green onion around the skinny part of the appetizer.

nutty holiday popcorn

Prep Time: 45 minutes   (Ready in 1 hour 15 minutes)

4 quarts (16 cups) popped popcorn

2 cups salted peanuts

¾ cup butter or margarine

⅓ cup sugar

1 (3-oz.) pkg. red or green gelatin

3 tablespoons water

1 tablespoon light corn syrup

1. Heat oven to 250°F. Cut two 8×12-inch sheets of foil. Place popcorn and peanuts in 2 ungreased 15×10×1-inch baking pans.

2. In medium saucepan, combine butter, sugar, gelatin, water and corn syrup. Cook over medium-low heat until sugar and gelatin are dissolved, stirring constantly. Using candy thermometer, continue cooking to 255°F. (hard-ball stage), stirring constantly. Pour syrup over popcorn and peanuts; stir to coat. (Mixture will be hot.)

3. Bake at 250°F. for 15 minutes. Stir mixture; bake an additional 10 minutes. Remove from oven; immediately turn mixture out of pans onto foil. Cool 30 minutes or until completely cooled. Break into small pieces. Store in tightly covered container.

Yield: 18 cups

NUTRITION INFORMATION PER SERVING
Serving Size: 1 Cup; Calories 290; Calories from Fat 180 **% Daily Value:** Total Fat 20g 31%; Saturated Fat 6g 30%; Cholesterol 20mg 7%; Sodium 130mg 5%; Total Carbohydrate 21g 7%; Dietary Fiber 3g 12%; Sugars 13g; Protein 6g; Vitamin A 6%; Vitamin C 0%; Calcium 2%; Iron 2% **Dietary Exchanges:** 1½ Starch, 4 Fat, 1½ Carbohydrate Choices

Special Touch

This pretty popcorn is perfect for presents (try saying *that* three times fast!). Why not fill several holiday-themed tins or jars to give as tasty gifts? Both kids and adults will love this crunchable munchable.

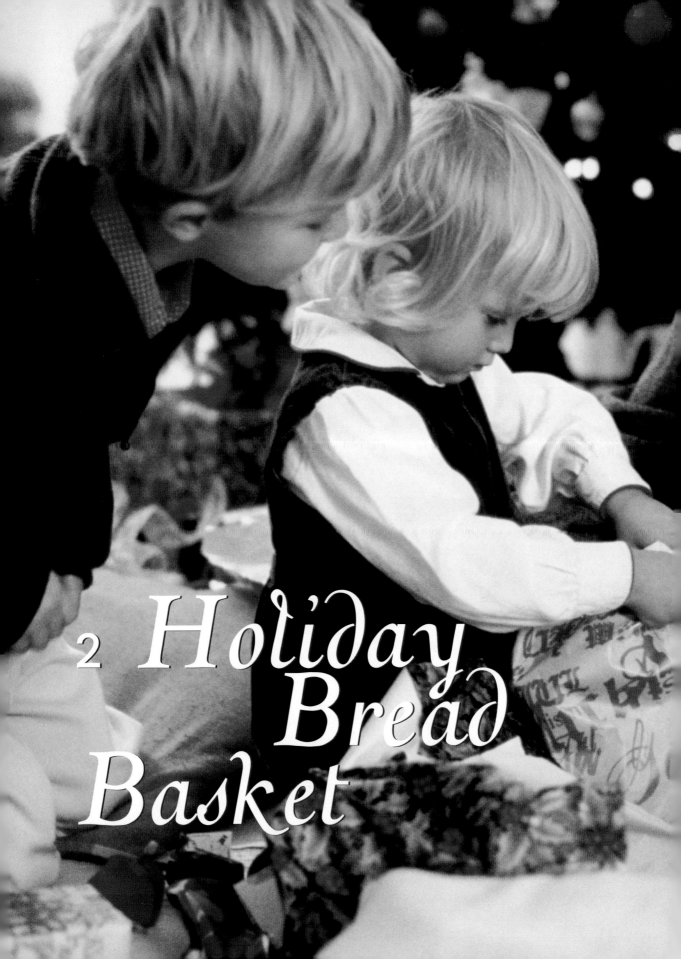

2 Holiday Bread Basket

Savory Nutty Crescents 46

Three-Cheese Crescent Pinwheels 47

Cranberry Upside-Down Muffins 49

Parmesan-Herb Muffins 50

Apple-Ginger Scones 52

Savory Cheese and Scallion Scones 54

Dill-Parmesan Popovers 55

Overnight Caramel-Apple Rolls 57

Crispy Onion Biscuits 58

Double-Chocolate Batter Bread 59

Dried Cherry-Cardamom Bread 61

Onion-Garlic Loaf 62

Holiday Focaccia 63

White Chocolate-Iced
Cranberry Bread 65

Danish Almond Crescent Ring 66

Sweet Nutcracker Braid 68

savory nutty crescents

2 tablespoons butter, softened

1 teaspoon dried sage leaves

1 (8-oz.) can refrigerated crescent dinner rolls

¼ cup chopped pecans

1. Heat oven to 375°F. In small bowl, combine butter and sage; mix well.

2. Separate dough into 8 triangles. Reserve 1 tablespoon butter mixture for topping. Spread remaining mixture evenly on triangles. Sprinkle each with pecans.

3. Roll up, starting at shortest side of each triangle, rolling to opposite point. Place on ungreased cookie sheet; curve each into crescent shape. Spread reserved butter mixture over tops of rolls.

4. Bake at 375°F. for 11 to 13 minutes or until golden brown. Serve warm.

Yield: 8 rolls

NUTRITION INFORMATION PER SERVING
Serving Size: 1 Roll; Calories 155; Calories from Fat 90 **% Daily Value:** Total Fat 10g 15%; Saturated Fat 3g 15%; Cholesterol 10mg 3%; Sodium 360mg 15%; Total Carbohydrate 14g 5%; Dietary Fiber 0g 0%; Sugars 4g; Protein 2g; Vitamin A 2%; Vitamin C 0%; Calcium 0%; Iron 4% **Dietary Exchanges:** 1 Starch, 2 Fat, 1 Carbohydrate Choice

Substitution

It's easy to cater to nut lovers of all kinds when making these savory crescents. This recipe calls for chopped pecans, but toasted walnuts or hazelnuts also taste great when paired with sage.

three-cheese crescent pinwheels

Prep Time: 30 minutes

2 oz. (½ cup) crumbled blue cheese

1 oz. (¼ cup) shredded hot pepper Monterey Jack cheese

2 tablespoons cream cheese, softened

1 tablespoon mayonnaise

1 (8-oz.) can refrigerated crescent dinner rolls

2 teaspoons chopped fresh parsley

1. Heat oven to 375°F. Lightly spray cookie sheet with non-stick cooking spray. In small bowl, combine all cheeses and mayonnaise; mix until well blended and soft.

2. Unroll dough into 2 long rectangles; press perforations to seal. Spread cheese mixture evenly over rectangles. Starting at short sides, roll up each; pinch edges to seal. Cut each roll into 8 slices. Place cut side down on sprayed cookie sheet. Sprinkle each with parsley.

3. Bake at 375°F. for 12 to 15 minutes or until golden brown. Immediately remove from cookie sheet; cool 3 minutes. Serve warm.

Yield: 16 pinwheels; 8 servings

Family Ties
Kids will clamor for these cheesy pinwheels, although blue cheese may not be their favorite. If you're trying to tempt tiny taste buds, steer clear of French Roquefort and choose a milder blue cheese such as Danablu, Gorgonzola, Stilton or Maytag Blue.

NUTRITION INFORMATION PER SERVING
Serving Size: ⅛ of Recipe; Calories 165; Calories from Fat 90 **% Daily Value:** Total Fat 10g 15%; Saturated Fat 4g 20%; Cholesterol 15mg 5%; Sodium 480mg 20%; Total Carbohydrate 14g 5%; Dietary Fiber 0g 0%; Sugars 4g; Protein 5g; Vitamin A 2%; Vitamin C 0%; Calcium 6%; Iron 4% **Dietary Exchanges:** 1 Starch, ½ High-Fat Meat, 1 Fat, 1 Carbohydrate Choice

cranberry upside-down muffins

Prep Time: 15 minutes   (Ready in 35 minutes)

¾ cup whole-berry cranberry sauce

¼ cup firmly packed brown sugar

2 cups all-purpose flour

2 tablespoons sugar

3 teaspoons baking powder

½ teaspoon salt

1 cup skim milk

¼ cup vegetable oil

1 teaspoon grated orange peel

2 egg whites

1. Heat oven to 400°F. Place wire rack over sheet of waxed paper. Spray 12 medium muffin cups with nonstick cooking spray. Spoon 1 tablespoon cranberry sauce into each muffin cup. Top each with 1 teaspoon brown sugar.

2. In large bowl, combine flour, sugar, baking powder and salt; mix well. In small bowl, combine milk, oil, orange peel and egg whites; blend well. Add to flour mixture all at once; stir just until dry ingredients are moistened. Divide batter evenly over cranberries and brown sugar in muffin cups.

3. Bake at 400°F. for 14 to 18 minutes or until toothpick inserted in center comes out clean. Cool in pan for 1 minute. Run knife around edges of cups to loosen. Invert muffins onto wire rack over waxed paper; remove pan. Cool 5 minutes. Serve warm.

Yield: 12 muffins

NUTRITION INFORMATION PER SERVING
Serving Size: 1 Muffin; Calories 180; Calories from Fat 45 **% Daily Value:** Total Fat 5g 8%; Saturated Fat 0g 0%; Cholesterol 0mg 0%; Sodium 250mg 10%; Total Carbohydrate 31g 10%; Dietary Fiber 0g 0%; Sugars 14g; Protein 3g; Vitamin A 0%; Vitamin C 0%; Calcium 10%; Iron 6% **Dietary Exchanges:** 1 Starch, 1 Fat, 1 Other Carbohydrate, 2 Carbohydrate Choices

Special Touch

These delicious muffins will look even more appealing when served with orange slices and a sprig of mint.

parmesan-herb muffins

Prep Time: 30 minutes

2 cups all-purpose flour

¾ cup grated Parmesan cheese

1 tablespoon sugar

1½ teaspoons baking powder

½ teaspoon baking soda

½ teaspoon dried sage leaves,
crumbled

½ cup chopped fresh parsley

1¼ cups buttermilk

¼ cup butter or margarine,
melted

1 egg, slightly beaten

1. Heat oven to 400°F. Grease bottoms only of 12 medium muffin cups or line with paper baking cups. In large bowl, combine flour, cheese, sugar, baking powder, baking soda, sage and parsley; mix well.

2. Add buttermilk, butter and egg; stir just until dry ingredients are moistened. Divide batter evenly into greased muffin cups, filling each about ⅓ full.

3. Bake at 400°F. for 15 to 20 minutes or until toothpick inserted in center comes out clean. Immediately remove from pan. Serve warm.

Yield: 12 muffins

NUTRITION INFORMATION PER SERVING
Serving Size: 1 Muffin; Calories 165; Calories from Fat 65 **% Daily Value:** Total Fat 7g 11%; Saturated Fat 4g 20%; Cholesterol 35mg 12%; Sodium 290mg 12%; Total Carbohydrate 19g 6%; Dietary Fiber 0g 0%; Sugars 3g; Protein 6g; Vitamin A 8%; Vitamin C 2%; Calcium 16%; Iron 6% **Dietary Exchanges:** 1 Starch, ½ Lean Meat, 1 Fat, 1 Carbohydrate Choice

Special Touch
Store-bought grated Parmesan cheese will work in this recipe, but freshly grated Parmesan will give these muffins a livelier taste and is worth the extra effort. No fancy tools are needed; a fine-holed grater will do.

create a beautiful holiday centerpiece

1. Place pillar candles of graduated heights on a tray (the tray makes the centerpiece portable and protects the table from dripping wax).

2. Arrange fresh fruit such as grapes around the candles.

3. Tuck in painted pinecones, small gold balls and lemon leaves. (Lemon leaves are an inexpensive green available at the florist; they can be spray-painted gold.)

apple-ginger scones

Prep Time: 30 minutes   (Ready in 50 minutes)

scones

2 cups all-purpose flour

⅓ cup sugar

3 teaspoons baking powder

½ teaspoon salt

6 tablespoons butter, cut into pieces

½ cup finely chopped peeled apple

¼ cup finely chopped crystallized ginger

1 egg

½ cup whipping cream

½ teaspoon grated lemon peel

glaze

¾ cup powdered sugar

1 tablespoon fresh lemon juice

1. Heat oven to 400°F. Spray cookie sheet with nonstick cooking spray. In medium bowl, combine flour, sugar, baking powder and salt; mix well. With pastry blender or fork, cut in butter until mixture resembles coarse crumbs. Stir in apple and ginger.

2. Beat egg in small bowl. Add cream and lemon peel; blend well. Add to dry ingredients; stir just until moistened.

3. On floured surface, gently knead dough 5 or 6 times. Place dough on sprayed cookie sheet; press to form 8-inch round, about 1 inch thick. Cut into 8 wedges; separate wedges slightly.

4. Bake at 400°F. for 15 to 20 minutes or until light golden brown and center is set.

5. In small bowl, blend powdered sugar and lemon juice until smooth. Drizzle glaze over warm scones. Serve warm.

Yield: 8 scones

NUTRITION INFORMATION PER SERVING
Serving Size: 1 Scone; Calories 330; Calories from Fat 125 **% Daily Value:** Total Fat 14g 22%; Saturated Fat 9g 45%; Cholesterol 65mg 22%; Sodium 400mg 17%; Total Carbohydrate 46g 15%; Dietary Fiber 1g 4%; Sugars 21g; Protein 5g; Vitamin A 10%; Vitamin C 0%; Calcium 12%; Iron 10% **Dietary Exchanges:** 2 Starch, 2½ Fat, 1 Other Carbohydrate, 3 Carbohydrate Choices

Family Ties

Weather and season permitting, why not take the family on an apple-picking adventure? Braeburn, Gala, Granny Smith and Haralson apples are all good "picks" because they won't add too much moisture to the scones.

savory cheese and scallion scones

Prep Time: 25 minutes   (Ready in 55 minutes)

scones

2¾ cups all-purpose flour

5 teaspoons baking powder

½ teaspoon salt, if desired

4 oz. (1 cup) crumbled feta cheese

4 oz. cream cheese, cut into 1-inch cubes

4 scallions or green onions, chopped

1 egg

1 cup half-and-half or milk

glaze, if desired

1 egg

2 tablespoons milk

1. Heat oven to 400°F. Grease large cookie sheet. In large bowl, combine flour, baking powder and salt; mix well. With pastry blender or fork, cut in feta cheese and cream cheese until mixture is crumbly. Add scallions; toss gently until combined.

2. Beat 1 egg in small bowl. Add half-and-half; blend well. Add to flour mixture; stir just until a soft dough forms.

3. On well-floured surface, gently knead dough 5 or 6 times. Pat or press dough into 1-inch-thick round. With floured knife, cut round into 8 wedges. Place wedges 2 inches apart on greased cookie sheet.

4. In small bowl, beat 1 egg and milk until well blended. Brush over tops of scones.

5. Bake at 400°F. for 25 to 30 minutes or until golden brown. Remove from cookie sheet, cool 3 minutes. Serve warm or cool. Store in refrigerator.

Yield: 8 scones

NUTRITION INFORMATION PER SERVING
Serving Size: 1 Scone; Calories 295; Calories from Fat 115 **% Daily Value:** Total Fat 13g 20%; Saturated Fat 8g 40%; Cholesterol 65mg 22%; Sodium 530mg 22%; Total Carbohydrate 36g 12%; Dietary Fiber 1g 4%; Sugars 3g; Protein 9g; Vitamin A 10%; Vitamin C 0%; Calcium 30%; Iron 14% **Dietary Exchanges:** 2½ Starch, 2½ Fat, 2½ Carbohydrate Choices

Special Touch

Sesame seed makes a tasty topping for these easy cheesy scones. Sprinkle some on the top of each egg-glazed biscuit before baking.

dill-parmesan popovers

Prep Time: 10 minutes   (Ready in 1 hour)

3 eggs, room temperature

1¼ cups milk, room temperature

1¼ cups all-purpose flour

2 tablespoons grated Parmesan cheese

1 teaspoon dried dill weed

½ teaspoon salt

1. Heat oven to 450°F. Generously grease 8 popover cups or 6-oz. custard cups. In small bowl, beat eggs with eggbeater or wire whisk until lemon colored and foamy. Add milk; blend well.

2. Add all remaining ingredients; beat with eggbeater just until batter is smooth and foamy on top. Pour batter evenly into greased cups, filling each about ⅓ full.

3. Bake at 450°F. for 20 minutes. (DO NOT OPEN OVEN.) Reduce oven temperature to 350°F.; bake an additional 15 to 30 minutes or until deep golden brown. Remove from oven; insert sharp knife into each popover to allow steam to escape. Remove from cups. Serve warm.

Yield: 8 popovers

Substitution
Sage is a great-tasting substitution for the dill in this recipe. If you like, you can flavor the batter with ½ teaspoon dried sage instead of the dill. Regardless of the herb you choose, there's little chance you'll have leftovers.

NUTRITION INFORMATION PER SERVING
Serving Size: 1 Popover; Calories 120; Calories from Fat 25 **% Daily Value:** Total Fat 3g 5%; Saturated Fat 1g 5%; Cholesterol 85mg 28%; Sodium 220mg 9%; Total Carbohydrate 17g 6%; Dietary Fiber 0g 0%; Sugars 2g; Protein 6g; Vitamin A 4%; Vitamin C 0%; Calcium 8%; Iron 6% **Dietary Exchanges:** 1 Starch, ½ Medium-Fat Meat, 1 Carbohydrate Choice

overnight caramel-apple rolls

Prep Time: 35 minutes   (Ready in 10 hours 30 minutes)

rolls

3 to 3½ cups all-purpose flour

¼ cup sugar

1 teaspoon salt

1 pkg. active dry yeast

½ cup applesauce

½ cup milk

¼ cup butter

1 egg

topping

½ cup firmly packed brown sugar

½ cup applesauce

3 tablespoons butter, melted

filling

2 tablespoons butter, softened

⅓ cup sugar

1 teaspoon cinnamon

1. In large bowl, combine 1 cup of the flour, ¼ cup sugar, the salt and yeast; mix well.

2. In small saucepan, heat ½ cup applesauce, the milk and ¼ cup butter over medium heat until very warm (120 to 130°F.), stirring constantly. Add warm mixture and egg to flour mixture; beat with electric mixer at low speed until moistened. Beat 2 minutes at medium speed. By hand, stir in 1½ to 1¾ cups flour until dough pulls cleanly away from sides of bowl.

3. On floured surface, knead in an additional ½ to ¾ cup flour until dough is smooth and elastic, about 5 minutes. Place dough in greased bowl; cover loosely with greased plastic wrap and cloth towel. Let rise in warm place (80 to 85°F.) until light and doubled in size, 45 to 60 minutes.

4. Grease 13×9-inch pan. Combine all topping ingredients in pan; mix well. Spread evenly in pan.

5. On lightly floured surface, roll dough to 15×12-inch rectangle. Spread dough with 2 tablespoons butter. In small bowl, combine ⅓ cup sugar and cinnamon; mix well. Sprinkle over butter.

6. Starting with 15-inch side, roll up tightly, pinching edges to seal. Cut roll into 12 slices; place cut side down over topping in pan. Cover; refrigerate at least 8 hours or overnight.

7. When ready to bake, let rolls stand at room temperature for 30 to 60 minutes. Heat oven to 400°F. Uncover rolls; bake 20 to 25 minutes or until golden brown. Cool in pan for 1 minute. Invert rolls onto serving tray; remove pan. Scrape any remaining topping onto rolls. Serve warm.

Yield: 12 rolls

NUTRITION INFORMATION PER SERVING
Serving Size: 1 Roll; Calories 300; Calories from Fat 90 **% Daily Value:** Total Fat 10g 15%; Saturated Fat 6g 30%; Cholesterol 40mg 13%; Sodium 270mg 11%; Total Carbohydrate 48g 16%; Dietary Fiber 1g 4%; Sugars 23g; Protein 4g; Vitamin A 8%; Vitamin C 0%; Calcium 2%; Iron 10% **Dietary Exchanges:** 1 Starch, 2 Fat, 2 Other Carbohydrate, 3 Carbohydrate Choices

crispy onion biscuits

Prep Time: 30 minutes

6 frozen buttermilk biscuits (from 25-oz. pkg.)

1 egg white, beaten

⅓ cup french-fried onions (from 2.8-oz. can), crushed

1. Heat oven to 375°F. Place frozen biscuits on ungreased cookie sheet, sides touching. Brush tops with beaten egg white. Top each with onions.

2. Bake at 375°F. for 20 to 24 minutes or until golden brown. Serve warm.

Yield: 6 biscuits

NUTRITION INFORMATION PER SERVING
Serving Size: 1 Biscuit; Calories 210; Calories from Fat 100 % **Daily Value:** Total Fat 11g 17%; Saturated Fat 3g 15%; Cholesterol 0mg 0%; Sodium 620mg 26%; Total Carbohydrate 23g 8%; Dietary Fiber 0g 0%; Sugars 3g; Protein 5g; Vitamin A 0%; Vitamin C 0%; Calcium 4%; Iron 6% **Dietary Exchanges:** 1½ Starch, 2 Fat, 1½ Carbohydrate Choices

Substitution
This recipe calls for frozen buttermilk biscuits, but other frozen biscuit varieties such as Cheddar garlic or southern-style are fun to try as well. Because the biscuits come in a resealable bag, you can make as few or as many as you like—simply adjust the amount of topping ingredients as needed.

double-chocolate batter bread

Prep Time: 30 minutes   (Ready in 2 hours 40 minutes)

3½ cups all-purpose flour

⅓ cup unsweetened cocoa

⅓ cup sugar

¼ teaspoon salt

¼ teaspoon baking soda

1 pkg. active dry yeast

1½ cups buttermilk

¼ cup butter

2 eggs

1 (12-oz.) pkg. (2 cups) semisweet chocolate chips

2 teaspoons oil

1. Generously grease 12-cup bundt cake pan. In large bowl, combine 2½ cups of the flour, the cocoa, sugar, salt, baking soda and yeast; mix well. In small saucepan, heat buttermilk and butter until very warm (120 to 130°F.). Add warm liquid and eggs to flour mixture; beat with electric mixer at low speed until moistened. Beat 3 minutes at high speed.

2. By hand, stir in remaining 1 cup flour and 1½ cups of the chocolate chips. Spoon dough evenly into greased pan. Cover with plastic wrap and cloth towel. Let rise in warm place (80 to 85°F.) until light and doubled in size, 30 to 40 minutes.

3. Heat oven to 350°F. Uncover dough; bake 35 to 45 minutes or until toothpick inserted near center comes out clean. Immediately invert bread onto wire rack; remove pan. Cool 45 minutes or until completely cooled.

4. Place remaining ½ cup chocolate chips and oil in resealable freezer plastic bag; seal bag. Knead bag to evenly distribute oil. Microwave on High for 30 to 60 seconds or until melted. Cut small hole in bottom corner of bag. Squeeze bag to drizzle melted chocolate over cooled bread.

Yield: 1 (12-slice) loaf

Special Touch

With a name like "Double-Chocolate," this bread, made with cocoa and chocolate chips, is a chocolate-lover's dream. To give as a gift, wrap a cooled loaf in festive colored cellophane and tie with a colorful ribbon. Don't forget to include the recipe.

dried cherry-cardamom bread

Prep Time: 25 minutes   (Ready in 3 hours 15 minutes)

¾ cup sugar

½ cup butter, softened

1 teaspoon vanilla

1 cup buttermilk

2 eggs

2 cups all-purpose flour

1 cup dried cherries, chopped

1 teaspoon grated lemon peel

½ teaspoon baking powder

½ teaspoon baking soda

½ teaspoon salt

½ teaspoon cardamom

1. Heat oven to 350°F. Spray bottom only of 9×5- or 8×4-inch loaf pan with nonstick cooking spray. In large bowl, combine sugar and butter; beat until light and fluffy. Beat in vanilla. Add buttermilk and eggs; blend well. (Mixture will appear curdled.)

2. In small bowl, combine all remaining ingredients; mix well. Add to buttermilk mixture; stir just until dry ingredients are moistened. Pour batter into sprayed pan.

3. Bake at 350°F. until toothpick inserted in center comes out clean. Bake 9×5-inch pan for 50 to 65 minutes; bake 8×4-inch pan for 55 to 75 minutes. Run knife around edges of pan to loosen bread; cool in pan on wire rack for 15 minutes. Remove bread from pan; place on wire rack. Cool 1½ hours or until completely cooled. Wrap tightly and store in refrigerator.

Yield: 1 (16-slice) loaf

Do-Ahead

This is a great bread to have on hand for last-minute holiday entertaining. Let the bread cool completely, then wrap it tightly with plastic wrap. Place the wrapped bread in a plastic food-storage freezer bag and freeze. One hour before serving, slice the frozen bread and arrange it on a platter.

NUTRITION INFORMATION PER SERVING
Serving Size: 1 Slice; Calories 185; Calories from Fat 65 **% Daily Value:** Total Fat 7g 11%; Saturated Fat 4g 20%; Cholesterol 45mg 15%; Sodium 190mg 8%; Total Carbohydrate 28g 9%; Dietary Fiber 0g 0%; Sugars 16g; Protein 3g; Vitamin A 4%; Vitamin C 0%; Calcium 2%; Iron 4% **Dietary Exchanges:** 1 Starch, 1 Fat, 1 Other Carbohydrate, 2 Carbohydrate Choices

onion-garlic loaf

Prep Time: 20 minutes   (Ready in 50 minutes)

1 tablespoon butter

½ cup thinly sliced green onions, including tops

1 garlic clove, minced

1 (11-oz.) can refrigerated French loaf

¼ cup grated Parmesan cheese

1. Heat oven to 350°F. Spray cookie sheet with nonstick cooking spray. Melt butter in small skillet over medium heat. Add onions and garlic; cook and stir 2 to 3 minutes or until tender.

2. Carefully unroll dough. Spread onion mixture evenly over dough. Reserve 1 teaspoon of the cheese for topping; sprinkle remaining cheese over onion mixture. Roll up dough; place seam side down on sprayed cookie sheet.

3. With sharp or serrated knife, make 4 or 5 diagonal slashes on top of loaf. Sprinkle with reserved 1 teaspoon cheese.

4. Bake at 350°F. for 26 to 30 minutes or until deep golden brown. Immediately remove from cookie sheet; cool 10 minutes. Cut diagonally into slices with serrated knife. Serve warm.

Yield: 5 servings

NUTRITION INFORMATION PER SERVING
Serving Size: ⅕ of Recipe; Calories 195; Calories from Fat 55 **% Daily Value:** Total Fat 6g 9%; Saturated Fat 3g 15%; Cholesterol 10mg 3%; Sodium 480mg 20%; Total Carbohydrate 28g 9%; Dietary Fiber 1g 4%; Sugars 3g; Protein 7g; Vitamin A 4%; Vitamin C 0%; Calcium 8%; Iron 8% **Dietary Exchanges:** 2 Starch, 1 Fat, 2 Carbohydrate Choices

Special Touch
Looking to add a little spice to your life? Try sprinkling fresh basil or dried oregano over the filling before rolling up the loaf.

holiday focaccia

Prep Time: 30 minutes   (Ready in 2 hours 40 minutes)

3 to 3¾ cups all-purpose flour

5 tablespoons sugar

1 teaspoon salt

1 teaspoon grated lemon peel

½ teaspoon cardamom

1 pkg. active dry yeast

1 cup warm water
(120 to 130°F.)

2 tablespoons vegetable oil

½ cup chopped candied
cherries or mixed fruit

⅓ cup coarsely chopped
almonds

¼ cup dried currants or raisins

1 tablespoon butter, melted

1. In large bowl, combine 1½ cups of the flour, 3 tablespoons of the sugar, the salt, lemon peel, cardamom and yeast; mix well. Add water and oil; beat 2 minutes at medium speed.

2. By hand, stir in cherries, almonds, currants and 1½ cups flour. If necessary, add remaining ¼ to ¾ cup flour until dough pulls away cleanly from sides of bowl.

3. On lightly floured surface, knead dough 5 to 10 times. Place in sprayed bowl; turn dough to grease top. Cover with sprayed plastic wrap and cloth towel. Let rise in warm place (80 to 85°F.) until doubled in size, 45 to 60 minutes.

4. Spray cookie sheet with nonstick cooking spray. Remove dough from bowl; lightly knead to form round ball. With sprayed hands, stretch and press dough to form 12-inch round. Place on sprayed cookie sheet. Brush with melted butter. Prick dough several times with fork. Cover; let rise in warm place until light and doubled in size, 40 to 50 minutes.

5. Heat oven to 400°F. Uncover dough; sprinkle with remaining 2 tablespoons sugar. Bake at 400°F. for 15 to 20 minutes or until golden brown. Immediately remove from cookie sheet; place on serving tray. Cool 10 minutes. With pizza cutter or serrated knife, cut focaccia into wedges. Serve warm.

Yield: 12 servings

NUTRITION INFORMATION PER SERVING
Serving Size: ¹⁄₁₂ of Recipe; Calories 215; Calories from Fat 45 % Daily Value: Total Fat 5g 8%; Saturated Fat 1g 5%; Cholesterol 5mg 2%; Sodium 230mg 10%; Total Carbohydrate 38g 13%; Dietary Fiber 1g 4%; Sugars 12g; Protein 4g; Vitamin A 0%; Vitamin C 0%; Calcium 2%; Iron 10% Dietary Exchanges: 1½ Starch, 1 Fat, 1 Other Carbohydrate, 2½ Carbohydrate Choices

Substitution

Don't feel limited to candied cherries, almonds and currants in this recipe. Feel free to incorporate your favorite nuts, dried fruits and candied fruits. Dried apricots are yummy with almonds, and figs and dates paired with walnuts are a tasty trio.

white chocolate-iced cranberry bread

Prep Time: 30 minutes   (Ready in 2 hours 30 minutes)

bread

2¼ cups all-purpose flour

¾ cup sugar

1½ teaspoons baking powder

½ teaspoon baking soda

½ teaspoon salt

½ cup coarsely chopped sweetened dried cranberries

¾ cup half-and-half

2 teaspoons grated orange peel

2 eggs

½ cup butter or margarine, melted

¼ cup orange juice

icing

1 oz. white chocolate baking bar, chopped

1 to 2 tablespoons half-and-half

½ cup powdered sugar

1. Heat oven to 350°F. Grease bottom only of 8×4-inch loaf pan. In large bowl, combine flour, sugar, baking powder, baking soda and salt; mix well. Stir in cranberries.

2. In small bowl, combine ¾ cup half-and-half, orange peel and eggs; beat well. Add half-and-half mixture, melted butter and orange juice to flour mixture; stir just until dry ingredients are moistened. Pour batter into greased pan.

3. Bake at 350°F. for 50 to 60 minutes or until deep golden brown and toothpick inserted in center comes out clean. Cool in pan for 10 minutes. Run knife around edges of pan to loosen loaf. Remove from pan; place on wire rack. Cool 1 hour or until completely cooled.

4. In small microwave-safe bowl, combine chocolate baking bar and 1 tablespoon of the half-and-half. Microwave on High for 30 seconds; stir until melted and smooth. If necessary, microwave an additional 10 to 20 seconds. With wire whisk, beat in powdered sugar until smooth. If necessary, add additional half-and-half, ½ teaspoon at a time, until of desired consistency. Spoon and spread icing over cooled loaf, allowing some to run down sides.

Yield: 1 (12-slice) loaf

Special Touch
Bake once, give three gifts! To make three mini loaves, grease bottoms only of three 5¾ × 3¼ × 2-inch foil loaf pans. Divide batter evenly into greased pans, using about 1 cup batter for each. Place the filled pans on a cookie sheet. Bake at 350°F. for 35 to 45 minutes or until golden brown and toothpick inserted in center comes out clean.

NUTRITION INFORMATION PER SERVING
Serving Size: 1 Slice; Calories 285; Calories from Fat 100 **% Daily Value:** Total Fat 11g 17%; Saturated Fat 7g 35%; Cholesterol 65mg 22%; Sodium 280mg 12%; Total Carbohydrate 42g 14%; Dietary Fiber 0g 0%; Sugars 24g; Protein 4g; Vitamin A 8%; Vitamin C 2%; Calcium 6%; Iron 6% **Dietary Exchanges:** 1 Starch, 2 Fat, 2 Other Carbohydrates, 3 Carbohydrate Choices

danish almond crescent ring

Prep Time: 20 minutes   (Ready in 45 minutes)

¼ cup sugar

3 tablespoons butter or margarine, softened

3½ oz. almond paste, broken into pieces

1 (8-oz.) can refrigerated crescent dinner rolls

1 egg, beaten

2 teaspoons sugar

2 to 4 tablespoons sliced almonds

1. Heat oven to 375°F. Lightly grease cookie sheet. In small bowl, combine sugar, butter and almond paste with fork until well mixed. Set aside.

2. Unroll dough into 2 long rectangles. Overlap long sides ½ inch to form 1 large rectangle; firmly press perforations and edges to seal. Press or roll to form 16×9-inch rectangle. Cut rectangle lengthwise into 3 equal strips.

3. Spoon 3 tablespoons almond paste mixture evenly down center of each strip. Gently press filling to form 1-inch-wide strip. Fold sides of dough over filling; firmly pinch edges to seal.

4. On greased cookie sheet, loosely braid the 3 filled strips. Shape braid into ring; pinch ends of strips together to seal. Brush with beaten egg. Sprinkle with 2 teaspoons sugar and the almonds.

5. Bake at 375°F. for 15 to 22 minutes or until golden brown. Cool 5 minutes. Remove from cookie sheet. Serve warm.

Yield: 8 servings

NUTRITION INFORMATION PER SERVING
Serving Size: ⅛ of Recipe; Calories 245; Calories from Fat 115 **% Daily Value:** Total Fat 13g 20%; Saturated Fat 4g 20%; Cholesterol 40mg 13%; Sodium 380mg 16%; Total Carbohydrate 28g 9%; Dietary Fiber 1g 4%; Sugars 17g; Protein 4g; Vitamin A 4%; Vitamin C 0%; Calcium 2%; Iron 6% **Dietary Exchanges:** 1 Starch, 2½ Fat, 1 Other Carbohydrate, 2 Carbohydrate Choices

Special Touch
This decorative bread is sure to draw "oohs" and "aahs" the instant it's removed from the oven—or possibly even sooner due to its wonderful aroma. When it is placed on a decorative tray or in a flat basket lined with holiday linen, folks will never know it was a snap to make.

stained-glass bag

1. Cut out desired holiday shape from a white note card.

2. On one side of a colored bag, trace around outer edge of the note card.

3. Cut bag ¼ inch inside traced line so opening is slightly smaller than note card.

4. Glue note card edged over cutout opening on bag.

5. Decorate around edge of cutout and note card with glitter paint; let dry.

6. Attach colored or clear plastic wrap over cutouts on inside of bag, using double-sided tape. Attach bow.

sweet nutcracker braid

Prep Time: 20 minutes   (Ready in 1 hour)

⅓ cup chopped pecans

½ cup finely chopped dates

¼ cup raisins

1 tablespoon sugar

⅛ teaspoon cinnamon

1 sheet frozen puff pastry, thawed

⅓ cup apricot preserves

¾ cup powdered sugar

¼ teaspoon vanilla

1 to 2 tablespoons milk

¼ cup chopped pecans

1. Heat oven to 375°F. Spray large cookie sheet with nonstick cooking spray. In small bowl, combine ⅓ cup pecans, the dates, raisins, sugar and cinnamon; mix well.

2. Unfold puff pastry; place on sprayed cookie sheet. With rolling pin, roll to form 14×10-inch rectangle. Spread preserves in 4-inch-wide strip lengthwise down center of pastry. Sprinkle fruit and nut mixture over preserves.

3. With scissors or sharp knife, make cuts 1 inch apart on long sides of pastry to within ½ inch of filling. Fold strips at an angle across filling mixture, overlapping ends and alternating from side to side. (See diagram on page 95.)

4. Bake at 375°F. for 20 to 25 minutes or until golden brown. Immediately remove from cookie sheet; place on serving tray. Cool 15 minutes.

5. In small bowl, blend powdered sugar, vanilla and enough milk for desired drizzling consistency. Drizzle over cooled braid. Sprinkle with ¼ cup pecans.

Yield: 8 servings

Do-Ahead

This sweet bread can be prepared and frozen up to four days ahead. Just make the recipe as directed, but hold off on glazing it. Let the braid cool, then wrap it tightly in plastic wrap. Seal it in a plastic food-storage bag and place in the freezer. When you're ready to serve, unwrap the braid and thaw it at room temperature before glazing it.

NUTRITION INFORMATION PER SERVING
Serving Size: ⅛ of Recipe; Calories 390; Calories from Fat 180 **% Daily Value:** Total Fat 20g 31%; Saturated Fat 4g 20%; Cholesterol 30mg 10%; Sodium 70mg 3%; Total Carbohydrate 48g 16%; Dietary Fiber 2g 8%; Sugars 31g; Protein 4g; Vitamin A 0%; Vitamin C 0%; Calcium 2%; Iron 10% **Dietary Exchanges:** 1 Starch, 4 Fat, 2 Other Carbohydrates, 3 Carbohydrate Choices

3 Casual
Get-Together
Meals

Slow-Cooked Beef Burgundy 73

Beef Fondue and Dipping Sauces 74

Spinach Pesto Manicotti 76

Oven-Roasted Pork Chops
and Vegetables 78

Beef, Bacon and Barley Soup 80

Sausage and Egg Brunch Bake 82

Make-Ahead Scrambled Eggs 83

Pizza Lasagna 85

Creamy Chicken-Vegetable Chowder 86

Chicken and Sausage Stew 87

Party Chicken Cacciatore 89

Skillet Chicken and Winter
Vegetables 90

Crescent Chicken Newburg 92

Overnight Chicken Enchilada Bake 93

Turkey and Ham Crescent Braid 95

Lemon and Herb-Roasted
Turkey Breast 96

Turkey with Italian Roasted
Vegetables 98

Seafood and Cheese Brunch Bake 100

Festive Oyster Stew 102

Chipotle-Black Bean Chili 103

Herbed Alfredo Sauce over Linguine 104

Winter Portobello Ratatouille 105

Menu Ideas for Casual Holiday Get-Togethers

Christmas Day Brunch

Serves 12

Orange Juice
Make-Ahead Scrambled Eggs, page 83
Hash Brown Potatoes
Fresh Fruit Platter
Overnight Caramel-Apple Rolls, page 57
Holiday Focaccia, page 63
Coffee and/or Tea

Ice-Skating Supper

Serves 8

Chili Cheese Dip and Potato Wedges,
    page 20
Overnight Chicken Enchilada Bake, page 93
Black Beans and Rice
Corn Muffins
Quick Saucy Cranberry Cake, page 171
Soft Drinks and/or Cold Beer

Cozy Holiday Supper

Serves 6

Creamy Chicken-Vegetable Chowder,
    page 86
Crispy Onion Biscuits, page 58
Lettuce Wedge with Ranch Dressing
Spiced Chocolate Crinkles, page 202

Christmas Turkey Dinner

Serves 8

Saucy Sausage Medallions, page 26
Lemon and Herb-Roasted Turkey Breast,
    page 96
Garlic Smashed Red Potatoes, page 153
Parmesan-Garlic Butter Green Beans
    (double recipe), page 145
Mediterranean Fennel Salad, page 157
Crescent Rolls
Cranberry-Apple Streusel Pie, page 175
Milk, Coffee and/or Tea

Christmas Eve Dinner

Serves 12

Fried Ravioli with Tomato Sauce, page 37
Breadsticks
Spinach Pesto Manicotti (double recipe),
    page 76
Italian Mixed Green Salad, page 155
White Chocolate-Raspberry Bars, page 209
Milk, Coffee and/or Tea

Kids'–Pick Dinner

Serves 8

Celery Sticks with Peanut Butter and Raisins
Pizza Lasagna, page 85
Jiggle Bell Salad, page 161
Santa Grahams, page 250

Tree-Trimming Appetizer Party

Serves 8 to 10

Assorted Cheeses with Crackers
Beef Tenderloin and Caramelized Onion
    Sandwiches, page 22
Teriyaki Seafood-Stuffed Mushrooms,
    page 30
Pork Tenderloin Crostini, page 24
Nutty Holiday Popcorn, page 43
Creamy Peppermint-Topped Brownie
    Dessert, page 195
Sparkling Cider and/or Eggnog

Post-Shop-'Til-You-Drop Party

Serves 10

Pastrami and Pepper Roll-ups, page 19
Party Chicken Cacciatore, page 89
Italian Bread
Caesar Salad
Christmas Cutouts, page 200
Caramel Candy Bars, page 214
Red Wine, Bottled Water, Coffee and/or Tea

slow-cooked beef burgundy

Prep Time: 20 minutes   (Ready in 12 hours 20 minutes)

⅓ cup all-purpose flour

1 teaspoon salt

¼ teaspoon pepper

2 lb. cubed beef stew meat

1½ cups fresh baby carrots, cut in half crosswise

1 (10-oz.) pkg. (3 cups) fresh pearl onions, peeled

1 (8-oz.) pkg. fresh small whole mushrooms

1 garlic clove, minced

1 bay leaf

1 (10½-oz.) can condensed beef consommé

1 cup water

½ cup red Burgundy wine

1. In 3½- to 4-quart slow cooker, combine flour, salt, pepper and beef stew meat; mix well. Add all remaining ingredients; mix well.

2. Cover; cook on Low setting for 10 to 12 hours.

Yield: 5 (1⅓-cup) servings

NUTRITION INFORMATION PER SERVING
Serving Size: 1⅓ Cups; Calories 450; Calories from Fat 190 **% Daily Value:** Total Fat 21g 32%; Saturated Fat 8g 40%; Cholesterol 110mg 37%; Sodium 850mg 35%; Total Carbohydrate 17g 6%; Dietary Fiber 2g 8%; Sugars 5g; Protein 41g; Vitamin A 100%; Vitamin C 6%; Calcium 4%; Iron 30% **Dietary Exchanges:** 1 Starch, 1 Vegetable, 5 Lean Meat, 1½ Fat, 1 Carbohydrate Choice

Family Ties
This hearty beef dish not only provides a satisfying meal for your family, but also gives you the gift of time. While it quietly simmers in your slow cooker, you can shop for gifts, decorate the tree, spend time with your kids or just take a breather from the holiday hustle and bustle.

beef fondue and dipping sauces

Prep Time: 20 minutes

aïoli dip

½ cup mayonnaise

1 large garlic clove, minced

3 tablespoons olive oil

¼ teaspoon salt

curry dip

¾ cup mayonnaise

1 teaspoon lemon juice

2 teaspoons curry powder

⅛ teaspoon ground ginger

horseradish sauce

⅓ cup mayonnaise

⅓ cup sour cream

1 tablespoon prepared horseradish

1 tablespoon Dijon mustard

steak sauce

½ cup ketchup

2 tablespoons Worcestershire sauce

½ teaspoon garlic salt

fondue

1 quart (4 cups) peanut oil

1 (3-lb.) beef tenderloin, cut into 1½-inch cubes

8 oz. fresh whole mushrooms

1. To prepare aïoli dip, in small bowl, combine mayonnaise and garlic; blend well. With wire whisk, beat in olive oil and salt until well blended.

2. To prepare curry dip, in small bowl, combine all ingredients; blend well.

3. To prepare horseradish sauce, in small bowl, combine all ingredients; blend well.

4. To prepare steak sauce, in small bowl, combine all ingredients; blend well. Cover each dip or sauce tightly. Refrigerate until serving time.

5. At serving time, heat peanut oil in fondue pot over medium heat until oil reaches 350°F. Place on warmer to maintain heat. Place beef cubes and mushrooms on serving platters.

6. Pass beef and mushrooms to guests. Place 1 or 2 pieces beef and/or mushrooms on fondue fork. Place in hot oil; cook until beef is of desired doneness and mushrooms are tender. Serve with dips and sauces.

Yield: 8 servings

NUTRITION INFORMATION PER SERVING
Serving Size: ⅛ of Recipe; Calories 315; Calories from Fat 160 % Daily Value: Total Fat 18g 28%; Saturated Fat 6g 30%; Cholesterol 95mg 32%; Sodium 90mg 4%; Total Carbohydrate 1g 1%; Dietary Fiber 0g 0%; Sugars 0g; Protein 37g; Vitamin A 2%; Vitamin C 0%; Calcium 0%; Iron 18% Dietary Exchanges: 5 Lean Meat, 1 Fat, 0 Carbohydrate Choice

Substitution

A less expensive cut of beef, such as boneless beef top sirloin steak, can be substituted for the beef tenderloin.

spinach pesto manicotti

Prep Time: 35 minutes   (Ready in 1 hour 15 minutes)

8 oz. uncooked manicotti

1 lb. extra-lean ground beef

1 (9-oz.) pkg. frozen spinach in a pouch, thawed, squeezed to drain and chopped

4 oz. (1 cup) diced mozzarella cheese

½ cup purchased pesto

1 egg

Dash salt

Dash pepper

1 (30-oz.) jar tomato pasta sauce

1. Heat oven to 400°F. Spray 13×9-inch (3-quart) glass baking dish with nonstick cooking spray. Cook manicotti as directed on package. Drain; rinse with cold water to cool. Drain well.

2. Meanwhile, in large bowl, combine ground beef, spinach, cheese, pesto and egg. If desired, add salt and pepper; mix well. For easier stuffing, place beef mixture in resealable freezer plastic bag. Seal bag; cut off 1 corner.

3. Fill each cooked manicotti by squeezing beef mixture into manicotti; place in sprayed baking dish. Pour pasta sauce over manicotti. Cover with foil.

4. Bake at 400°F. for 30 to 40 minutes or until beef filling is no longer pink in center.

Yield: 6 servings

NUTRITION INFORMATION PER SERVING
Serving Size: ⅙ of Recipe; Calories 620; Calories from Fat 260 % **Daily Value:** Total Fat 29g 45%; Saturated Fat 9g 45%; Cholesterol 95mg 32%; Sodium 1200mg 50%; Total Carbohydrate 59g 20%; Dietary Fiber 4g 16%; Sugars 12g; Protein 31g; Vitamin A 74%; Vitamin C 20%; Calcium 30%; Iron 28% **Dietary Exchanges:** 3 Starch, 3 Medium-Fat Meat, 2½ Fat, 1 Other Carbohydrate, 4 Carbohydrate Choices

Special Touch
For an elegant yet easy garnish, top this delicious manicotti with shavings of fresh Parmigiano-Reggiano cheese. All you need is a wedge of the cheese and a vegetable peeler. Be forewarned—the cheese is a bit on the pricey side, but it's well worth the burst of flavor it provides.

oh, mini tree

1. Fill miniature flowerpots with florist's oasis.

2. Add a cone-shaped piece of oasis to the top of each pot.

3. Insert small sprigs of fresh or artificial greenery (we used dwarf Alberta spruce). Spritz the fresh greenery with water.

4. Decorate with miniature ornaments, jingle bells or ribbon bows. Set one "tree" at each table setting.

oven-roasted pork chops and vegetables

Prep Time: 15 minutes   (Ready in 1 hour 10 minutes)

2 tablespoons frozen apple juice concentrate

1 tablespoon olive or vegetable oil

1 tablespoon Dijon mustard

½ teaspoon seasoned salt

½ teaspoon dried marjoram leaves

½ teaspoon garlic-pepper blend

4 (½-inch-thick) bone-in center-cut pork chops, trimmed of fat

1½ cups fresh baby carrots

1 medium red onion, cut into 8 wedges

2 cups frozen whole green beans

1. Heat oven to 425°F. Spray 15×10×1-inch baking pan with nonstick cooking spray. In large bowl, combine apple juice concentrate, oil, mustard, seasoned salt, marjoram and garlic-pepper blend; mix well.

2. Brush pork chops with about half of oil mixture; set pork aside. Add carrots and onion to remaining oil mixture; toss to coat. Arrange carrots and onion in sprayed pan. Bake at 425°F. for 15 minutes.

3. Remove pan from oven. Add green beans; stir gently to mix. Arrange pork chops on vegetable mixture.

4. Return to oven; bake an additional 30 to 40 minutes or until pork chops are no longer pink in center and vegetables are fork-tender. Serve pork and vegetables with pan drippings.

Yield: 4 servings

NUTRITION INFORMATION PER SERVING
Serving Size: ¼ of Recipe; Calories 250; Calories from Fat 100 **% Daily Value:** Total Fat 11g 17%; Saturated Fat 3g 15%; Cholesterol 60mg 20%; Sodium 330mg 14%; Total Carbohydrate 15g 5%; Dietary Fiber 3g 12%; Sugars 8g; Protein 23g; Vitamin A 100%; Vitamin C 6%; Calcium 6%; Iron 10% **Dietary Exchanges:** ½ Fruit, 1 Vegetable, 3 Lean Meat, ½ Fat, ½ Other Carbohydrate, 1 Carbohydrate Choice

Substitution

If you're lucky enough to live in a climate where you have access to fresh green beans during the winter, go ahead and use them instead of the frozen. The green beans as well as the carrots in this recipe are great ways to get vitamins A and C.

beef, bacon and barley soup

Prep Time: 25 minutes   (Ready in 8 hours 25 minutes)

4 slices bacon, cut into ½-inch pieces

1½ lb. boneless beef round steak, cut into ½-inch pieces

1 medium onion, chopped (½ cup)

4 small red potatoes, unpeeled, cut into ½-inch cubes (about 2 cups)

1½ cups fresh baby carrots, cut in half lengthwise

1 cup frozen whole kernel corn

½ cup uncooked regular pearl barley

2 (14-oz.) cans beef broth

1 (14.5-oz.) can diced tomatoes with basil, garlic and oregano, undrained

1 (12-oz.) jar beef gravy

1. Cook bacon in large nonstick skillet over medium-high heat for 3 minutes, stirring frequently. Add beef and onion; cook 3 to 5 minutes or until beef is browned, stirring occasionally.

2. In 3½- to 4-quart slow cooker, layer potatoes, carrots, corn and barley. Top with beef mixture. Pour broth, tomatoes and gravy over top. Do not stir.

3. Cover; cook on low setting for 7 to 8 hours. Stir before serving.

Yield: 8 (1½-cup) servings

Family Ties

As this soup slowly simmers and the ingredients release their flavors in your slow cooker, head outside and build a snowman or create snow angels with your kids. You won't believe the mouthwatering smells you'll return to when you come inside. A sip of this comforting soup will warm you up, from the inside out, in no time.

NUTRITION INFORMATION PER SERVING
Serving Size: 1½ Cups; Calories 260; Calories from Fat 55 **% Daily Value:** Total Fat 6g 9%; Saturated Fat 2g 10%; Cholesterol 50mg 17%; Sodium 860mg 36%; Total Carbohydrate 32g 11%; Dietary Fiber 5g 20%; Sugars 4g; Protein 24g; Vitamin A 88%; Vitamin C 12%; Calcium 4%; Iron 18% **Dietary Exchanges:** 2 Starch, 2½ Very Lean Meat, 1 Fat, 2 Carbohydrate Choices

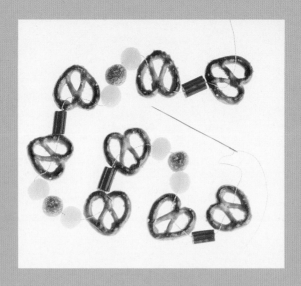

pretzel and candy garland

1. On threaded needle using heavy colored thread, string 8 small pretzel twists (through top 2 holes), 4 licorice bites and small gumdrops as shown above.

2. Knot thread at each end to secure. (Remove thread before eating.) Makes 1 (21-inch) garland.

sausage and egg brunch bake

Prep Time: 40 minutes (Ready in 9 hours 50 minutes)

egg bake

1½ lb. bulk Italian pork sausage

5 cups frozen country-style shredded hash-brown potatoes (from 30-oz. pkg.)

½ cup sliced green onions

2 (4.5-oz.) jars sliced mushrooms, drained

1 (2¼-oz.) can sliced ripe olives, drained

1 tablespoon chopped fresh basil

12 oz. (3 cups) shredded colby-Monterey Jack cheese blend

8 eggs

1½ cups milk

½ teaspoon salt

topping

1 tablespoon olive or vegetable oil

1 garlic clove, minced

6 Italian plum tomatoes, chopped (about 2 cups)

¼ teaspoon salt

2 tablespoons chopped fresh basil

1. Spray 13×9-inch (3-quart) glass baking dish and 16×12-inch sheet of foil with nonstick cooking spray. Cook sausage in large skillet over medium-high heat until no longer pink, stirring occasionally. Remove sausage from skillet; drain on paper towels.

2. In large bowl, combine potatoes, onions, mushrooms, olives, 1 tablespoon basil and 2 cups of the cheese. Add cooked sausage; stir gently to mix. Spoon evenly into sprayed baking dish. Sprinkle with remaining 1 cup cheese.

3. Beat eggs in same large bowl. Add milk and ½ teaspoon salt; beat well. Pour over potato mixture in baking dish. Cover with sprayed foil. Refrigerate at least 8 hours or overnight.

4. To serve, heat oven to 350°F. Bake covered for 45 minutes. Uncover baking dish; bake an additional 20 to 25 minutes or until center is set. Let stand 10 minutes before serving.

5. Meanwhile, heat oil in medium skillet over medium heat until hot. Add garlic; cook and stir 1 minute. Add tomatoes and ¼ teaspoon salt; cook about 5 minutes or until tomatoes are tender, stirring occasionally. Stir in 2 tablespoons basil.

6. To serve, cut egg bake into squares. Serve with warm topping.

Yield: 12 servings

Substitution
Try this egg bake with shredded hot pepper Monterey Jack or mozzarella cheese instead of the colby-Monterey Jack cheese blend.

make-ahead scrambled eggs

Prep Time: 40 minutes

8 slices bacon

1 (8-oz.) pkg. (3 cups) sliced fresh mushrooms

3 tablespoons butter or margarine

16 eggs

1 cup half-and-half or milk

½ teaspoon salt

¼ teaspoon pepper

1 (10¾-oz.) can condensed cream of mushroom soup

2 tablespoons chopped fresh chives

4 Italian plum tomatoes, quartered, sliced

8 oz. (2 cups) shredded Cheddar cheese

1. In 12-inch nonstick skillet, cook bacon until crisp. Drain on paper towels. Crumble bacon; set aside. Reserve 1 table-spoon bacon drippings in skillet. Add mushrooms to drip-pings; cook 4 to 5 minutes or until tender, stirring frequently. Remove from skillet; set aside. Wipe skillet clean with paper towel.

2. Melt butter in same skillet over medium heat. Beat eggs in large bowl. Add half-and-half, salt and pepper; beat well. Add egg mixture to skillet; cook over medium heat until firm but still moist, stirring occasionally. Stir in soup and chives.

3. Place half of egg mixture in 3½- to 4-quart slow cooker. Top with half of each of the cooked mushrooms, tomatoes, cheese and crumbled bacon. Repeat layers.

4. Serve immediately, or cover and keep warm on Low setting for up to 4 hours.

Yield: 12 (¾-cup) servings

NUTRITION INFORMATION PER SERVING
Serving Size: ¾ Cup; Calories 280; Calories from Fat 200 **% Daily Value:** Total Fat 22g 34%; Saturated Fat 11g 55%; Cholesterol 320mg 107%; Sodium 570mg 24%; Total Carbohydrate 5g 2%; Dietary Fiber 0g 0%; Sugars 3g; Protein 16g; Vitamin A 18%; Vitamin C 2%; Calcium 16%; Iron 8% **Dietary Exchanges:** 2½ High-Fat Meat, ½ Fat, 0 Carbohydrate Choice

Special Touch
Scrambled eggs from a slow cooker? Bet you didn't even know it was possible. Before serving, sprinkle a few chopped fresh chives and diced plum tomato pieces on top. An additional sprinkle of cheese never hurts, either.

pizza lasagna

Prep Time: 45 minutes   (Ready in 1 hour 20 minutes)

9 uncooked lasagna noodles

1 (15-oz.) can pizza sauce

1 (14½-oz.) can diced tomatoes with green pepper and onion, undrained

1 (15-oz.) container ricotta cheese

1 teaspoon dried Italian seasoning

8 oz. (2 cups) shredded mozzarella cheese

2 (3½-oz.) pkg. pepperoni slices

1 (4.5-oz.) jar sliced mushrooms, drained

1 (2¼-oz.) can sliced ripe olives, drained

½ cup chopped green bell pepper

2 tablespoons grated Parmesan cheese

1. Cook lasagna noodles as directed on package. Drain.

2. Meanwhile, heat oven to 350°F. Spray 12×8-inch (2-quart) glass baking dish with nonstick cooking spray. In medium saucepan, combine pizza sauce and tomatoes; cook until thoroughly heated.

3. In medium bowl, combine ricotta cheese and Italian seasoning; mix well.

4. Spread ¼ cup sauce mixture in sprayed baking dish. Arrange 3 cooked noodles over sauce in dish. Spoon and spread half of ricotta mixture over noodles. Top with ½ cup mozzarella cheese, 1 cup sauce, ⅓ each of the pepperoni, mushrooms, olives and bell pepper. Repeat layers once. Top with remaining 3 noodles, sauce, mozzarella cheese, pepperoni, mushrooms, olives and bell pepper. Sprinkle with Parmesan cheese.

5. Bake at 350°F. for 30 to 35 minutes or until lasagna is bubbly. Let stand 10 minutes before serving.

Yield: 8 servings

NUTRITION INFORMATION PER SERVING
Serving Size: ⅛ of Recipe; Calories 435; Calories from Fat 215 **% Daily Value:** Total Fat 24g 37%; Saturated Fat 10g 50%; Cholesterol 55mg 18%; Sodium 1350mg 56%; Total Carbohydrate 31g 10%; Dietary Fiber 2g 8%; Sugars 7g; Protein 24g; Vitamin A 18%; Vitamin C 20%; Calcium 42%; Iron 14% **Dietary Exchanges:** 2 Starch, 2½ Medium-Fat Meat, 2 Fat, 2 Carbohydrate Choices

Family Ties

Lasagna and pizza—now *that's* a kid-friendly combination made in heaven! If your kids are picky eaters, you may want to leave out the mushrooms, olives and bell pepper in this recipe or choose different vegetables more to their liking.

creamy chicken-vegetable chowder

Prep Time: 25 minutes

chowder

1½ cups milk or half-and-half

1 cup chicken broth

1 (10¾-oz.) can condensed cream of potato soup

1 (10¾-oz.) can condensed cream of chicken soup

2 cups cubed cooked chicken or turkey

⅓ cup chopped green onions

1 (11-oz.) can vacuum-packed whole kernel corn with red and green peppers, drained

1 (4.5-oz.) jar sliced mushrooms, drained

1 (4.5-oz.) can chopped green chiles

6 oz. (1½ cups) shredded Cheddar cheese

crescent rolls

1 (8-oz.) can refrigerated crescent dinner rolls

¼ cup crushed nacho-flavored tortilla chips

1. In 4-quart saucepan or Dutch oven, combine milk, broth, potato soup and chicken soup; blend well. Add all remaining chowder ingredients except cheese; mix well. Cook over medium heat for 5 to 8 minutes or until onions are tender, stirring occasionally. Remove from heat. Add cheese; stir until melted.

2. While chowder is heating, bake crescent rolls. Heat oven to 375°F. Shape dough as directed on can. Gently press top of each roll in crushed chips. Place on ungreased cookie sheet.

3. Bake at 375°F. for 11 to 13 minutes or until golden brown. Serve chowder with crescent rolls.

Yield: 6 servings

Special Touch

This chowder looks gussied up when garnished with sliced green onions and nacho-flavored tortilla chips. And for best results, remember to keep refrigerated dough refrigerated right up until you're ready to use it.

chicken and sausage stew

Prep Time: 30 minutes

1 tablespoon vegetable oil

3 boneless skinless chicken thighs, cut into bite-sized pieces

1 medium carrot, chopped

1 medium onion, chopped

1 medium stalk celery, chopped

1 cup frozen whole kernel corn

1 teaspoon cumin

1 (15-oz.) can tomato sauce

1 (14.5-oz.) can diced tomatoes, undrained

4 oz. fully cooked smoked sausage, cut into thin slices

¼ cup grated Parmesan cheese, if desired

1. Heat oil in large saucepan or Dutch oven over medium-high heat until hot. Add chicken, carrot, onion and celery; cook 5 minutes, stirring frequently.

2. Stir in all remaining ingredients except cheese. Bring to a boil. Reduce heat; cover and simmer 5 to 10 minutes or until chicken is no longer pink in center and vegetables are tender. Sprinkle with cheese.

Yield: 4 (1½-cup) servings

Substitution

If you don't happen to have chicken thighs on hand, you can use two boneless chicken breasts instead. And when it comes to the smoked sausage, use your favorite. Polish, reduced-fat beef or venison sausages are tasty options to use in this hearty stew.

chipotle-black bean chili

Prep Time: 20 minutes

1 large onion, chopped (1 cup)

4 garlic cloves, minced

3 (15-oz.) cans black beans, drained, rinsed

1 (28-oz.) can whole tomatoes, undrained, cut up

1 (14.5-oz.) can diced tomatoes, undrained

2 chipotle chiles in adobo sauce (from 7- or 11-oz. can), finely chopped

1½ teaspoons dried oregano leaves

¾ teaspoon cumin

1. Spray nonstick Dutch oven with nonstick cooking spray. Heat over medium heat until hot. Add onion and garlic; cover and cook 4 minutes, stirring occasionally.

2. Add all remaining ingredients; mix well. Bring to a boil. Reduce heat; cover and simmer 8 to 10 minutes to blend flavors, stirring occasionally.

Yield: 6 (1½-cup) servings

NUTRITION INFORMATION PER SERVING
Serving Size: 1½ Cups; Calories 310; Calories from Fat 20 **% Daily Value:** Total Fat 2g 3%; Saturated Fat 0g 0%; Cholesterol 0mg 0%; Sodium 1170mg 49%; Total Carbohydrate 68g 23%; Dietary Fiber 16g 64%; Sugars 12g; Protein 21g; Vitamin A 16%; Vitamin C 30%; Calcium 22%; Iron 36% **Dietary Exchanges:** 3 Starch, 1 Vegetable, 1½ Very Lean Meat, 3½ Carbohydrate Choices

Family Ties
Set out bowls of shredded Cheddar cheese, sour cream, chopped green onions and chopped fresh tomatoes, and let everyone at the table personalize their own meal.

herbed alfredo sauce over linguine

Prep Time: 30 minutes

2 (9-oz.) pkg. refrigerated linguine or 12 oz. uncooked linguine

2 teaspoons butter or margarine

1 teaspoon olive oil

3 large garlic cloves, minced

½ cup finely chopped red bell pepper

⅓ cup sliced green onions

⅓ cup chopped fresh parsley or 3 teaspoons dried parsley flakes

¼ cup all-purpose flour

2 (12 oz.) cans evaporated low fat 2% milk

1 teaspoon dried basil leaves

½ teaspoon dried oregano leaves

½ teaspoon salt

⅓ cup grated Parmesan cheese

1. Cook linguine in Dutch oven as directed on package. Drain; return to Dutch oven and cover to keep warm.

2. Meanwhile, in large nonstick skillet, melt butter with oil over medium heat. Add garlic; cook and stir 1 minute. Add bell pepper, onions, parsley and flour; cook and stir 1 minute.

3. Gradually stir in milk until well blended. Bring to a boil, stirring constantly. Cook 6 to 10 minutes or until sauce is bubbly and thickened, stirring frequently.

4. Remove skillet from heat. Stir in basil, oregano and salt. Pour sauce over linguine; toss gently to coat. Sprinkle with cheese.

Yield: 5 (1½-cup) servings

NUTRITION INFORMATION PER SERVING
Serving Size: 1½ Cups; Calories 390; Calories from Fat 100 **% Daily Value:** Total Fat 11g 17%; Saturated Fat 6g 30%; Cholesterol 35mg 12%; Sodium 690mg 29%; Total Carbohydrate 53g 18%; Dietary Fiber 2g 8%; Sugars 19g; Protein 20g; Vitamin A 38%; Vitamin C 30%; Calcium 54%; Iron 14% **Dietary Exchanges:** 2½ Starch, 1 Low-Fat Milk, ½ Lean Meat, 1 Fat, 3½ Carbohydrate Choices

winter portobello ratatouille

Prep Time: 50 minutes   (Ready in 2 hours 20 minutes)

4 tablespoons olive oil

2 large onions, sliced

4 large garlic cloves, minced

2 (6-oz.) pkg. portobello mushrooms, gills removed, cubed

2 large eggplants, peeled, cut into bite-sized chunks

3 medium zucchini, quartered lengthwise, cut into ¾-inch chunks (about 4 cups)

¼ cup chopped fresh basil

1 teaspoon salt

1 teaspoon dried thyme leaves

½ teaspoon pepper

1 (28-oz.) can diced tomatoes, undrained

1. Heat oven to 350°F. Heat 2 tablespoons of the oil in Dutch oven over medium heat until hot. Add onions; cook and stir 3 minutes. Add garlic; cook and stir 1 to 2 minutes or until tender. Add mushrooms; cook 3 to 5 minutes or until tender, stirring frequently. Remove vegetables from Dutch oven; set aside.

2. Heat remaining 2 tablespoons oil in same Dutch oven over medium heat until hot. Add eggplants and zucchini; cook 6 to 8 minutes or until tender, stirring occasionally. Add basil, salt, thyme and pepper; mix well. Stir in tomatoes. Return onion and mushroom mixture to Dutch oven; mix well. Cover.

3. Bake at 350°F. for 45 minutes. Uncover Dutch oven; bake an additional 45 minutes or until vegetables are very tender. If desired, sprinkle with shredded fresh Parmesan cheese.

Yield: 10 (1⅓-cup) servings

Do-Ahead

You can make this veggie-filled ratatouille a day ahead. Simply refrigerate it and bake it the next day if you like. If you have an aluminum Dutch oven, make sure to transfer it to a glass bowl first, because the aluminum will react with the diced tomatoes.

NUTRITION INFORMATION PER SERVING
Serving Size: 1⅓ Cups; Calories 120; Calories from Fat 55 **% Daily Value:** Total Fat 6g 9%; Saturated Fat 1g 5%; Cholesterol 0mg 0%; Sodium 360mg 15%; Total Carbohydrate 18g 6%; Dietary Fiber 5g 20%; Sugars 9g; Protein 4g; Vitamin A 18%; Vitamin C 18%; Calcium 4%; Iron 10% **Dietary Exchanges:** 3 Vegetable, 1 Fat, 1 Carbohydrate Choice

4 *Christmas Day Entrées*

Peppered Steak with Brandy-Mushroom Sauce 109

Steak Neapolitan 110

Peppered Beef Tenderloin with Wine Sauce 111

Pepper-Crusted Prime Rib with Zinfandel Sauce 113

Prime Rib-Eye Roast 114

Baked Ham with Zesty Cranberry Sauce 116

Pineapple-Orange Glazed Ham 117

Glazed Crown Roast with Cranberry-Cornbread Stuffing 119

Spice and Herb-Roasted Pork Tenderloin 120

Fennel-Garlic Pork Roast 122

Apple-Glazed Pork Chops with Sage-Apple Stuffing 123

Pesto and Pepper-Stuffed Leg of Lamb 125

Honey-Mustard Roasted Chicken and Squash 126

Stuffed Roast Turkey and Gravy 128

Cherry-Balsamic Cornish Hen with Rice 130

Roast Goose with Chestnut-Prune Stuffing 132

Roasted Orange-Fennel Halibut with Dijon Sauce 133

Deviled Lobster Tails 134

Italian Roasted Salmon 136

Bagel 'n Brie Brunch Strata 137

Elegant Holiday Menus

Baked Ham Christmas Dinner

Serves 12

Cherry-Cheese Spread, page 40
Baked Ham with Zesty Cranberry Sauce,
    page 116
Honey-Mustard Dilled Brussels Sprouts
    (triple recipe), page 141
Festive Coleslaw with Citrus Vinaigrette,
    page 162
Eggnog Bread Pudding with Cherry-Bourbon
    Sauce, page 193
Coffee and Milk

Festive French Twist Dinner

Serves 8

Winter Greens with Pomegranate-
    Champagne Vinaigrette, page 158
Peppered Beef Tenderloin with Wine Sauce,
    page 111
Three-Potato Gratin, page 149
Triple-Chocolate Truffle Trees, page 179
Sparkling Apple Cider and Champagne

Luxurious Lobster

Serves 4

White Wine Spritzer
Deviled Lobster Tails, page 134
Tarragon Green Peas, page 146
Dill-Parmesan Popovers, page 55
Individual Lemon-Lime Cream Tarts, page 180
Coffee and/or Tea

The Crowning Touch

Serves 12

Smoked Salmon on Endive, page 33
Glazed Crown Roast with Cranberry-
    Cornbread Stuffing, page 119
Broccoli with Walnut-Garlic Butter
    (double recipe), page 140

Merlot Wine
Mocha Truffle Cheesecake, page 190
Coffee and Milk

Prime-Time Celebration

Serves 12

Goat Cheese and Olive Phyllo Purses, page 42
Pepper-Crusted Prime Rib with Zinfandel
    Sauce, page 113
Almond Baby Carrots (double recipe), page 143
Winter Fruit Salad, page 159
Savory Nutty Crescents, page 46
Orange Crème Dessert with Ruby Cranberry
    Sauce, page 182
Red Zinfandel Wine
Coffee and Milk

Christmas Day Brunch

Serves 8

Bagel 'n Brie Brunch Strata, page 137
Smoked Breakfast Sausage
Crisp Bacon Strips
Cranberry Upside-Down Muffins, page 49
Cantaloupe and Honeydew Melon Wedges
Orange Juice
Coffee and/or Tea

Turkey and All the Trimmings

Serves 12 to 16

Assorted Fresh Vegetables
Stuffed Roast Turkey and Gravy, page 128
Broccoli Spears
Sweet Potatoes with Apples and Onions
    (double recipe), page 147
Baked Brandied Cranberries (double recipe),
    page 163
Merlot Wine
Chocolate-Almond Mousse Cake, page 166
Milk, Coffee and/or Tea

peppered steak with brandy-mushroom sauce

Prep Time: 30 minutes

sauce

1 tablespoon unsalted butter

2 tablespoons finely chopped shallots

½ cup beef broth

¼ cup brandy or beef broth

¼ cup whipping cream

1 (4.5-oz.) jar whole mushrooms, drained

steak

1 (13-oz.) beef T-bone or rib steak (¾ inch thick)

2 teaspoons vegetable oil

1 tablespoon assorted whole peppercorns, crushed

1. Melt butter in small saucepan over medium-high heat. Add shallots; cook and stir 1 to 2 minutes or until tender.

2. Add all remaining sauce ingredients. Bring to a boil. Boil uncovered over medium-high heat for 15 to 20 minutes or until sauce is reduced to about ¾ cup, thickened and beige in color, stirring occasionally.

3. Brush both sides of steak with oil. Coat steak with peppercorns, pressing into steak. Place steak on broiler pan.

4. Broil 3 to 4 inches from heat for about 5 minutes or until steak is browned. Turn steak; broil 5 to 10 minutes or until of desired doneness. Serve sauce over steak.

Yield: 2 servings

NUTRITION INFORMATION PER SERVING
Serving Size: ½ of Recipe; Calories 485; Calories from Fat 300 **% Daily Value:** Total Fat 33g 51%; Saturated Fat 15g 75%; Cholesterol 150mg 50%; Sodium 370mg 15%; Total Carbohydrate 4g 1%; Dietary Fiber 1g 4%; Sugars 2g; Protein 43g; Vitamin A 14%; Vitamin C 2%; Calcium 4%; Iron 22% **Dietary Exchanges:** 6 Medium-Fat Meat, 1 Fat, 0 Carbohydrate Choice

Family Ties

If you're cooking this finger-licking-good dish for kids and adults, you may want to make this recipe twice. For the adults, simply make as directed, but for the kids you may want to use beef broth instead of the brandy.

steak neapolitan

Prep Time: 20 minutes

1 teaspoon vegetable oil

2 tablespoons lemon juice

4 (4-oz.) beef tenderloin steaks (about 1 inch thick)

1 cup finely chopped onions (2 medium)

1 cup dry Marsala wine

2 tablespoons chopped fresh Italian parsley

1. Heat oil in large skillet over medium-high heat until hot. Add lemon juice and steaks; cook 8 to 10 minutes or until of desired doneness, turning once. Remove steaks from skillet; cover to keep warm.

2. Add onions and wine to juice mixture in skillet; cook and stir 4 minutes or until liquid is reduced to about ½ cup.

3. To serve, spoon onion mixture over steaks. Sprinkle with parsley.

Yield: 4 servings

Steak Neapolitan pictured here with Tarragon Green Peas, page 146, and Italian Mixed Green Salad, page 155.

NUTRITION INFORMATION PER SERVING
Serving Size: ¼ of Recipe; Calories 290; Calories from Fat 90 **% Daily Value:** Total Fat 10g 15%; Saturated Fat 3g 15%; Cholesterol 65mg 22%; Sodium 65mg 3%; Total Carbohydrate 11g 4%; Dietary Fiber 1g 4%; Sugars 4g; Protein 25g; Vitamin A 6%; Vitamin C 6%; Calcium 2%; Iron 14% **Dietary Exchanges:** 3 Medium-Fat Meat, 1 Other Carbohydrate, 1 Carbohydrate Choice

peppered beef tenderloin
with wine sauce

Prep Time: 20 minutes   (Ready in 2 hours 35 minutes)

sauce

6 shallots (about 6 oz.)

1 small carrot, cut into ¼-inch pieces

1 teaspoon olive oil

1 (14-oz.) can beef broth

2 cups dry red wine

1 tablespoon tomato paste

1 teaspoon dried thyme leaves

1 bay leaf

tenderloin

1 (3½-lb.) beef tenderloin

1 tablespoon olive oil

1 tablespoon cracked black pepper

1. Heat oven to 400°F. Peel shallots; cut lengthwise into ¼-inch-wide slices. Place shallots and carrot in ungreased 13×9-inch pan. Add 1 teaspoon oil; toss to coat.

2. Bake at 400°F. for 20 to 25 minutes or until vegetables are tender.

3. Use small amount of broth to loosen any browned bits from bottom of pan; pour into large saucepan. Add roasted vegetables, remaining broth, the wine, tomato paste, thyme and bay leaf; blend well. Bring to a boil over medium-high heat. Cook 30 minutes or until reduced to about 2 cups (about half of total). Cool 30 minutes.

4. Remove bay leaf. In blender container, blend vegetables with liquid until pureed. Return to saucepan. Cover; refrigerate.

5. Increase oven temperature to 450°F. Place beef tenderloin in shallow metal roasting pan. Rub tenderloin with 1 tablespoon oil. Sprinkle top and sides with pepper. Place pan over medium-high heat; cook until tenderloin is browned on all sides. Place pan in 450°F. oven. Immediately reduce oven temperature to 375°F.; bake 40 to 50 minutes or until meat thermometer inserted in center registers 140°F.

6. Remove tenderloin from pan; cover with foil to keep warm. Add small amount of vegetable sauce to roasting pan; stir to loosen any browned bits. Bring remainder of vegetable sauce in saucepan to a boil, adding sauce from roasting pan. Cut tenderloin into slices. Serve with sauce.

Yield: 8 servings

NUTRITION INFORMATION PER SERVING
Serving Size: ⅛ of Recipe; Calories 385; Calories from Fat 145 **% Daily Value:** Total Fat 16g 25%; Saturated Fat 6g 30%; Cholesterol 115mg 38%; Sodium 350mg 15%; Total Carbohydrate 4g 1%; Dietary Fiber 1g 4%; Sugars 2g; Protein 44g; Vitamin A 26%; Vitamin C 2%; Calcium 2%; Iron 22% **Dietary Exchanges:** 6 Lean Meat, 0 Carbohydrate Choice

pepper-crusted prime rib with zinfandel sauce

Prep Time: 25 minutes   (Ready in 2 hours 10 minutes)

roast

1 (6-lb.) boneless prime or choice beef rib roast

3 garlic cloves, sliced

1 tablespoon mixed peppercorns, coarsely ground

1 tablespoon mustard seed

1 tablespoon Worcestershire sauce

1 tablespoon Dijon mustard

sauce

2 tablespoons finely chopped shallots

1 cup red Zinfandel wine

1 (14-oz.) can beef broth

¼ cup all-purpose flour

2 tablespoons brandy or beef broth

1 tablespoon chopped fresh parsley

1. Heat oven to 450°F. With tip of knife, make shallow slits in surface of beef roast. Insert slices of garlic. In small bowl, combine ground peppercorns, mustard seed, Worcestershire sauce and Dijon mustard; mix well. Spread over surface of roast. Place roast on rack in shallow metal roasting pan.

2. Bake at 450°F. for 15 minutes. Reduce oven temperature to 350°F.; bake an additional 1¼ to 1½ hours or until meat thermometer inserted in center registers 140°F. for medium-rare.

3. Remove roast from pan; cover with foil to keep warm. Remove and discard all but 2 tablespoons drippings from pan. Add shallots; cook and stir over medium heat for 2 to 3 minutes or until shallots are tender. Add wine; cook over medium-high heat until mixture boils, scraping brown bits from bottom of pan.

4. In small bowl, combine broth and flour; blend well. Stir into wine mixture. Cook until mixture comes to a boil, stirring frequently. Boil 3 minutes or until slightly thickened. Stir in brandy.

5. Cut roast into slices. Serve with sauce. Sprinkle individual servings with parsley.

Yield: 12 servings

Substitution

Red Zinfandel, a fruity wine, is a good match for this robust beef dish. Another fruity red wine, such as Cabernet Sauvignon or Pinot Noir, can be used in place of the red Zinfandel.

prime rib-eye roast

Prep Time: 10 minutes   (Ready in 4 hours)

½ cup dry red wine

¼ cup balsamic vinegar

2 tablespoons Worcestershire sauce

3 medium garlic cloves, minced

1½ teaspoons salt

½ teaspoon coarse ground black pepper

2 (5- to 5½-lb.) boneless beef small-end rib-eye roasts

1. In medium bowl, combine all ingredients except beef roasts; mix well. Divide marinade between 2 large resealable food storage plastic bags or two 12×8-inch (2-quart) glass baking dishes.

2. Add 1 beef roast to each bag or baking dish, turning to coat all sides. Seal bags or cover dishes with plastic wrap. Refrigerate 1 to 8 hours to marinate, turning occasionally.

3. To serve, heat oven to 350°F. Place beef roasts, fat side up, on racks in shallow roasting pans; discard marinade.

4. Bake at 350°F. for 1¾ to 2 hours for medium-rare or until meat thermometer inserted in center registers 135°F., or 2 to 2½ hours for medium doneness or until meat thermometer registers 150°F. Let roasts stand 15 to 20 minutes. Cut roasts into slices.

Yield. 12 servings

NUTRITION INFORMATION PER SERVING
Serving Size: ¹⁄₁₂ of Recipe; Calories 595; Calories from Fat 245 **% Daily Value:** Total Fat 27g 42%; Saturated Fat 10g 50%; Cholesterol 215mg 72%; Sodium 510mg 21%; Total Carbohydrate 1g 1%; Dietary Fiber 0g 0%; Sugars 1g; Protein 81g; Vitamin A 4%; Vitamin C 0%; Calcium 2%; Iron 40% **Dietary Exchanges:** 11 Lean Meat, 0 Carbohydrate Choice

Special Touch
Don't let the fact that this recipe calls for wine intimidate you. Simply use your favorite drinking wine, or get a recommendation from a liquor store. Both Merlot and Cabernet Sauvignon are good choices.

pet's paw box

1. Use an animal paw stamp and ink pad to make paw prints on a small square or round box. Let dry.

2. Spray clear acrylic sealer over box; let dry.

3. Fasten pet collar or ribbon around box, adjusting so box lid is secure.

4. Attach pet toys or treats to collar or ribbon.

baked ham with
zesty cranberry sauce

Prep Time: 20 minutes   (Ready in 2 hours 5 minutes)

ham

1 (6-lb.) fully cooked rump half, bone-in ham

sauce

1 (16-oz.) can jellied cranberry sauce

⅓ cup apple juice

¼ cup port wine

2 tablespoons lemon juice

1 tablespoon Dijon mustard

2 teaspoons sugar

2 teaspoons grated lemon peel

2 teaspoons grated orange peel

¼ teaspoon white pepper

¼ teaspoon ground ginger

1. Heat oven to 325°F. Place ham on rack in shallow roasting pan. Add ¼ to ½ inch water to pan. Cover pan.

2. Bake at 325°F. for 45 minutes. Uncover pan; bake an additional 45 minutes to 1¼ hours or until meat thermometer inserted in center, but not touching bone, registers 140°F.

3. In small saucepan, combine all sauce ingredients; mix well with wire whisk. Cook over medium heat for 10 minutes or until cranberry sauce is melted and mixture is thoroughly heated, stirring frequently. Cut ham into slices. Serve with sauce.

Yield: 12 servings

NUTRITION INFORMATION PER SERVING
Serving Size: ¹⁄₁₂ of Recipe; Calories 220; Calories from Fat 55 % **Daily Value:** Total Fat 6g 9%; Saturated Fat 2g 10%; Cholesterol 60mg 20%; Sodium 1350mg 56%; Total Carbohydrate 19g 6%; Dietary Fiber 0g 0%; Sugars 17g; Protein 23g; Vitamin A 0%; Vitamin C 0%; Calcium 0%; Iron 10% **Dietary Exchanges:** 1 Fruit, 3 Very Lean Meat, 1 Fat, 1 Carbohydrate Choice

Do-Ahead

You can cut down on the time you spend in the kitchen on Christmas Day by making this flavorful sauce the night before. When you're ready to use it, just heat before serving. The sauce also makes a thoughtful gift. Pour it into a decorative jar, and store in the refrigerator until you're ready to present it.

pineapple-orange glazed ham

Prep Time: 10 minutes   (Ready in 8 hours 10 minutes)

1 (3-lb.) boneless cooked ham

1 (8-oz.) can crushed pineapple in unsweetened juice

½ cup firmly packed brown sugar

3 tablespoons orange marmalade

1 teaspoon prepared mustard

1. Place ham in 3½- to 5-quart slow cooker. Drain pineapple liquid from can into slow cooker; refrigerate pineapple. In small bowl, combine brown sugar, 1 tablespoon of the marmalade and the mustard; mix well. Spread over ham.

2. Cover; cook on Low setting for 6 to 8 hours.

3. About 5 minutes before serving, in small microwave-safe bowl, combine pineapple and remaining 2 tablespoons orange marmalade; mix well. Microwave on High for 1¼ to 1½ minutes or until thoroughly heated, stirring once halfway through cooking.

4. Remove ham from slow cooker; place on cutting board. Cut ham into slices. Serve with pineapple mixture.

Yield: 10 servings

NUTRITION INFORMATION PER SERVING
Serving Size: ¹⁄₁₀ of Recipe; Calories 265; Calories from Fat 90 **% Daily Value:** Total Fat 10g 15%; Saturated Fat 4g 20%; Cholesterol 70mg 23%; Sodium 1750mg 73%; Total Carbohydrate 18g 6%; Dietary Fiber 0g 0%; Sugars 17g; Protein 26g; Vitamin A 0%; Vitamin C 2%; Calcium 2%; Iron 10% **Dietary Exchanges:** 3½ Lean Meat, 1 Other Carbohydrate, 1 Carbohydrate Choice

Special Touch
Personalizing this dish is as easy as choosing your favorite orange marmalade and/or mustard. If you don't have a favorite or like the idea of trying something new, check out specialty stores in your area for ideas.

glazed crown roast with cranberry-cornbread stuffing

Prep Time: 35 minutes   (Ready in 3 hours 35 minutes)

stuffing

3 (6-oz.) pkg. one-step cornbread stuffing mix

Butter or margarine

Water

¾ cup sweetened dried cranberries

¾ cup chopped dried apples

roast

1 (12-bone) pork crown roast (about 7 lb.)

¼ cup apple jelly

2 tablespoons jellied cranberry sauce

1. Heat oven to 350°F. In large saucepan, prepare stuffing mix as directed on package, using butter and water. Stir in cranberries and apples. Set aside.

2. Place pork roast on rack in shallow roasting pan. Fill cavity with as much of the prepared stuffing as it will hold. Cover stuffing and bones loosely with foil. Spray 1-quart casserole with nonstick cooking spray. Spoon remaining stuffing into sprayed casserole. Cover; refrigerate until 45 minutes before serving time.

3. Bake roast at 350°F. for 2¼ to 3 hours, allowing 25 to 30 minutes per pound, or until meat thermometer inserted in center registers 155°F.

4. Meanwhile, in small saucepan, combine apple jelly and cranberry sauce; mix well. Heat over low heat until mixture is melted and smooth.

5. During last 45 minutes of baking time, brush roast with jelly mixture and bake any remaining stuffing.

6. Remove roast from pan. Cover with foil; let stand 15 minutes. Remove string from roast; cut between bones. Serve with stuffing from center of roast and additional baked stuffing.

Yield: 12 servings

NUTRITION INFORMATION PER SERVING
Serving Size: ¹⁄₁₂ of Recipe; Calories 590; Calories from Fat 235 **% Daily Value:** Total Fat 26g 40%; Saturated Fat 12g 60%; Cholesterol 135mg 45%; Sodium 820mg 34%; Total Carbohydrate 48g 16%; Dietary Fiber 2g 8%; Sugars 14g; Protein 41g; Vitamin A 8%; Vitamin C 2%; Calcium 4%; Iron 16% **Dietary Exchanges:** 2 Starch, 1 Fruit, 5 Lean Meat, 2 Fat, 3 Carbohydrate Choices

Do-Ahead
Save yourself some time in the kitchen by serving this elegant holiday dish with Caesar salad from a bag and purchased dinner rolls. Using a scalloped potato mix also shortens cooking time.

spice and herb-roasted pork tenderloin

Prep Time: 15 minutes   (Ready in 50 minutes)

½ teaspoon garlic-pepper blend

½ teaspoon dried rosemary leaves, crushed

½ teaspoon dried thyme leaves, crushed

½ teaspoon paprika

¼ teaspoon salt

2 (¾-lb.) pork tenderloins

2 teaspoons olive or vegetable oil

1. Heat oven to 425°F. In small bowl, combine garlic-pepper blend, rosemary, thyme, paprika and salt; mix well.

2. Brush pork tenderloins with oil. Sprinkle with seasoning mixture; rub in with fingers. Place tenderloins in ungreased shallow baking pan.

3. Bake at 425°F. for 25 to 35 minutes or until meat thermometer inserted in center registers 160°F. Let stand 5 minutes before slicing.

Yield: 6 servings

NUTRITION INFORMATION PER SERVING
Serving Size: ⅙ of Recipe; Calories 160; Calories from Fat 55 **% Daily Value:** Total Fat 6g 9%; Saturated Fat 2g 10%; Cholesterol 70mg 23%; Sodium 150mg 6%; Total Carbohydrate 0g 0%; Dietary Fiber 0g 0%; Sugars 0g; Protein 26g; Vitamin A 2%; Vitamin C 0%; Calcium 0%; Iron 8% **Dietary Exchanges:** 4 Very Lean Meat, ½ Fat, 0 Carbohydrate Choice

Special Touch

For an extra-special presentation, slice this tenderloin on the diagonal before serving. Au gratin potatoes make a tasty side dish.

fennel-garlic pork roast

Prep Time: 10 minutes   (Ready in 1 hour 15 minutes)

1 (2½-lb.) rolled boneless pork loin roast

1 tablespoon fennel seeds

1 tablespoon chopped fresh thyme or 1 teaspoon dried thyme leaves

½ teaspoon salt

½ teaspoon coarse ground black pepper

2 tablespoons olive oil

3 garlic cloves, minced

1. Heat oven to 375°F. Place pork roast in shallow baking pan. In small bowl, combine all remaining ingredients; blend well. Spread mixture over roast.

2. Bake at 375°F. for 40 to 50 minutes or until pork is no longer pink in center and meat thermometer inserted in center registers 160°F.

3. Remove roast from pan. Cover with tent of foil; let stand 10 to 15 minutes. Remove string from roast; cut into slices.

Yield: 8 servings

NUTRITION INFORMATION PER SERVING
Serving Size: ⅛ of Recipe; Calories 265; Calories from Fat 135 **% Daily Value:** Total Fat 15g 23%; Saturated Fat 4g 20%; Cholesterol 90mg 30%; Sodium 200mg 8%; Total Carbohydrate 0g 0%; Dietary Fiber 0g 0%; Sugars 0g; Protein 32g; Vitamin A 0%; Vitamin C 0%; Calcium 2%; Iron 6% **Dietary Exchanges:** 5 Lean Meat, 0 Carbohydrate Choice

Family Ties
The taste of fennel is a matter of personal preference. If someone in your family isn't a big fan of the aromatic herb, adjust the amount as you see fit.

apple-glazed pork chops with sage-apple stuffing

Prep Time: 20 minutes   (Ready in 1 hour 30 minutes)

4 (1-inch-thick) boneless pork loin chops (about 1½ lb.)

1 tablespoon butter or margarine

½ cup chopped celery

½ cup chopped green onions

½ cup chopped apple

¼ cup raisins

¼ to ½ teaspoon dried sage leaves, crushed

2 cups sage and onion-seasoned stuffing cubes

3 tablespoons apple juice

½ teaspoon peppered seasoned salt

¼ cup apple jelly

1. Heat oven to 350°F. Cut deep horizontal pocket in side of each pork chop.

2. Melt butter in medium nonstick skillet over medium heat. Add celery and ¼ cup of the onions; cook and stir 2 to 3 minutes or until crisp-tender. Add apple, raisins and sage; mix well. Remove from heat. Stir in stuffing cubes and apple juice.

3. Stuff each pork chop with about ½ cup stuffing mixture. Place in ungreased 13×9-inch pan. Sprinkle pork chops with peppered seasoned salt. Arrange any remaining stuffing mixture around chops. Cover with foil.

4. Bake at 350°F. for 45 minutes. Meanwhile, in small saucepan, combine remaining ¼ cup onions and the jelly; heat over low heat until melted, stirring occasionally.

5. Uncover pork chops; brush with jelly mixture. Bake uncovered an additional 20 to 30 minutes or until pork chops are no longer pink in center, brushing with jelly mixture once or twice.

Yield: 4 servings

NUTRITION INFORMATION PER SERVING
Serving Size: ¼ of Recipe; Calories 425; Calories from Fat 110 **% Daily Value:** Total Fat 12g 18%; Saturated Fat 5g 25%; Cholesterol 75mg 25%; Sodium 790mg 33%; Total Carbohydrate 52g 17%; Dietary Fiber 3g 12%; Sugars 20g; Protein 27g; Vitamin A 4%; Vitamin C 4%; Calcium 6%; Iron 12% **Dietary Exchanges:** 2 Starch, ½ Fruit, 3 Lean Meat, 1 Other Carbohydrate, 3½ Carbohydrate Choices

Family Ties
This delicious dish is a great choice for casual entertaining—especially when kids are invited to the table. The apple-pork chop combo suits pint-sized palates. Older children can help chop ingredients and stuff the savory-sweet dressing into the chops.

pesto and pepper-stuffed leg of lamb

Prep Time: 15 minutes   (Ready in 1 hour 30 minutes)

pesto

¾ cup firmly packed fresh parsley

¼ cup fresh rosemary leaves

¼ cup fresh mint leaves

3 garlic cloves

2 tablespoons olive oil

lamb

1 (5-lb.) rolled boneless leg of lamb

1 (7.5-oz.) jar roasted red bell peppers, well drained

2 teaspoons lemon-pepper seasoning

1. Heat oven to 350°F. In food processor bowl with metal blade, combine all pesto ingredients; process until smooth.

2. Unroll lamb, cut side up, onto work surface. Spread pesto over lamb. Place roasted peppers over pesto. Roll up lamb. Tie with kitchen string or secure edges with metal skewers. Rub surface with lemon-pepper seasoning. Place on rack in shallow roasting pan.

3. Bake at 350°F. for 60 to 75 minutes or until meat thermometer inserted in center registers 145°F. for medium-rare. Remove string from lamb; cut into slices.

Yield: 12 servings

Do-Ahead

You have lots of options for getting a head start on making this dish. You can mix the pesto and refrigerate it overnight, and the roast can be stuffed, tied, covered and refrigerated for up to three hours. You can also skip making the pesto altogether and buy it instead.

honey-mustard roasted chicken and squash

Prep Time: 15 minutes   (Ready in 1 hour)

4 bone-in chicken breast halves, skin removed

1 medium butternut squash, peeled, cut into 1-inch cubes

1 medium red onion, cut into 8 wedges

¾ cup purchased light honey-mustard salad dressing

½ teaspoon salt

½ teaspoon dried rosemary leaves, crushed

¼ teaspoon garlic powder

2 cups frozen sugar snap peas (from 1-lb. pkg.)

1. Heat oven to 425°F. Spray 15×10×1-inch baking pan with nonstick cooking spray. Place chicken breast halves in sprayed pan. Arrange squash and onion around chicken.

2. In small bowl, combine salad dressing, salt, rosemary and garlic powder; blend well. Brush about half of salad dressing mixture over chicken and vegetables. Bake at 425°F. for 20 minutes.

3. Remove pan from oven. Stir vegetables; add sugar snap peas to pan. Brush remaining salad dressing mixture over chicken and vegetables.

4. Return to oven; bake an additional 20 to 25 minutes or until chicken is fork-tender, its juices run clear and vegetables are tender.

Yield: 4 servings

NUTRITION INFORMATION PER SERVING
Serving Size: ¼ of Recipe; Calories 345; Calories from Fat 125 **% Daily Value:** Total Fat 14g 22%; Saturated Fat 3g 15%; Cholesterol 75mg 25%; Sodium 720mg 30%; Total Carbohydrate 25g 8%; Dietary Fiber 4g 16%; Sugars 14g; Protein 30g; Vitamin A 100%; Vitamin C 40%; Calcium 8%; Iron 16% **Dietary Exchanges:** 1½ Starch, 1 Vegetable, 3 Lean Meat, 1 Fat, 1½ Carbohydrate Choices

Special Touch
Before serving, arrange the chicken and vegetables on an attractive serving platter and garnish with sprigs of fresh rosemary.

stuffed roast turkey and gravy

Prep Time: 30 minutes   (Ready in 5 hours)

turkey

1 (12- to 16-lb.) whole turkey, thawed if frozen

½ teaspoon salt

Stuffing of choice

⅓ cup butter or margarine, melted

gravy

Turkey pan drippings

2 (14-oz.) cans chicken broth

⅓ cup all-purpose flour

Water

1. Heat oven to 325°F. Remove and discard neck and giblets from turkey. Rinse turkey inside and out with cold water; pat dry with paper towels. Sprinkle cavity of turkey with salt.

2. Spoon stuffing loosely into neck and body cavities of turkey. Place any remaining stuffing in lightly buttered casserole; cover and refrigerate to bake as side dish. Turn wings back and tuck tips over shoulder joints. Refasten drumsticks with metal piece or tuck under skin at tail. Fasten neck skin to back with skewers.

3. Place turkey, breast side up, in roasting pan. Insert oven-proof meat thermometer so bulb reaches center of thickest part of thigh, but does not rest on bone. Spoon melted butter over turkey. Do not add water or cover.

4. Bake at 325°F. for 3½ to 4¼ hours or until thermometer registers 180 to 185°F. and leg joint moves easily. If necessary, cover turkey breast with tent of foil during last 1½ to 2 hours of baking to prevent excessive browning.

5. Remove turkey from pan; let stand 15 minutes. Remove skewers from turkey. Remove stuffing; place in serving bowl.

NUTRITION INFORMATION PER SERVING
Serving Size: 1/16 of Recipe; Calories 485; Calories from Fat 245 **% Daily Value:** Total Fat 27g 42%; Saturated Fat 9g 45%; Cholesterol 145mg 48%; Sodium 450mg 19%; Total Carbohydrate 16g 5%; Dietary Fiber 0g 0%; Sugars 0g; Protein 45g; Vitamin A 4%; Vitamin C 0%; Calcium 2%; Iron 16% **Dietary Exchanges:** 1 Starch, 6 Lean Meat, 2 Fat, 1 Carbohydrate Choice

6. Pour drippings from roasting pan into strainer over bowl. Spoon off fat that rises to top, reserving ½ cup fat. Pour drippings into measuring cup. Add broth and enough water to make 7 cups liquid. Set aside.

7. In large saucepan, combine reserved ½ cup fat and flour; mix well with wire whisk. Cook over medium heat for about 2 minutes or until mixture turns golden brown, stirring constantly with wire whisk.

8. Gradually stir drippings mixture into flour mixture. Cook over low heat until mixture boils and thickens, stirring constantly.

Yield: 12 to 16 servings turkey; 7 cups gravy

let it glow

1. Fill several straight-sided vases or jars with water.

2. Add fresh whole cranberries and small pine boughs or holly sprigs and/or mistletoe.

3. Top with a floating candle.

cherry-balsamic cornish hen with rice

Prep Time: 10 minutes   (Ready in 1 hour 10 minutes)

1 (24-oz.) Cornish game hen

1 (6-oz.) pkg. seasoned long-grain and wild rice mix

¼ cup dried cherries

3 tablespoons slivered almonds

1½ cups water

½ teaspoon garlic-pepper blend

¼ teaspoon salt

¼ cup cherry preserves

2 tablespoons balsamic vinegar

1. Heat oven to 375°F. Remove and discard neck and giblets from game hen. With kitchen scissors, cut game hen in half.

2. In ungreased 11×7-inch (2-quart) glass baking dish, combine rice with seasoning from package, cherries, almonds and water; mix well. Top with game hen halves, skin side up. Sprinkle with garlic-pepper blend and salt.

3. In small bowl, combine preserves and vinegar; mix well. Brush about half of mixture over game hen halves. Cover with foil.

4. Bake at 375°F. for 30 minutes. Uncover baking dish; brush game hen halves with remaining preserves mixture. Bake uncovered an additional 25 to 30 minutes or until game hen is fork-tender, its juices run clear and rice is tender.

Yield: 2 servings

NUTRITION INFORMATION PER SERVING
Serving Size: ½ of Recipe; Calories 805; Calories from Fat 360 **% Daily Value:** Total Fat 40g 62%; Saturated Fat 10g 50%; Cholesterol 240mg 80%; Sodium 430mg 18%; Total Carbohydrate 65g 22%; Dietary Fiber 3g 12%; Sugars 32g; Protein 46g; Vitamin A 4%; Vitamin C 4%; Calcium 6%; Iron 18% **Dietary Exchanges:** 3 Starch, 5 Medium-Fat Meat, 3 Fat, 1 Other Carbohydrate, 4 Carbohydrate Choices

Substitution

If you don't have any garlic-pepper blend on hand, you can use ¼ teaspoon garlic powder mixed with ¼ teaspoon coarsely ground pepper instead.

roast goose with
chestnut-prune stuffing

Prep Time: 30 minutes   (Ready in 3 hours 10 minutes)

goose

1 (8- to 9-lb.) whole goose

1 teaspoon salt

stuffing

¼ cup chopped onion

¼ cup chopped celery

1 cup chopped pitted prunes

1 (10-oz.) can peeled chestnuts, drained, quartered

3 cups cornbread stuffing mix

1 teaspoon salt

1 teaspoon allspice

¼ teaspoon pepper

1½ cups apple cider or juice

1. Heat oven to 450°F. Remove and discard neck, giblets and excess fat from goose. Rinse goose inside and out with cold water; pat dry with paper towels. Sprinkle cavity of goose with 1 teaspoon salt.

2. Spray large nonstick skillet with nonstick cooking spray. Heat over medium-high heat until hot. Add onion and celery; cook 3 to 4 minutes or until tender, stirring occasionally.

3. Stir in prunes and chestnuts. Cook 2 to 3 minutes or until thoroughly heated, stirring occasionally. Remove from heat. Add stuffing mix, 1 teaspoon salt, the allspice and pepper; mix lightly. Add apple cider; mix just until moistened.

4. Spoon stuffing loosely into cavity of goose; close cavity with metal skewers or sew shut with kitchen twine. Turn wings back and tuck tips under shoulder joints. Secure drumsticks with twine. Place goose, breast side up, on rack in shallow roasting pan. Pour enough boiling water into pan to just reach rack. Prick skin generously with meat fork. Do not cover.

5. Bake at 450°F. for 15 to 20 minutes or until goose begins to brown.

6. Reduce oven temperature to 350°F. Insert ovenproof meat thermometer so bulb reaches center of thickest part of thigh, but does not rest on bone. Bake an additional 1¾ to 2 hours or until thermometer registers 180 to 185°F., basting goose every 20 to 30 minutes with pan juices. Remove excess fat as it accumulates in pan. If necessary, cover goose with tent of foil to prevent excessive browning.

7. Remove goose from pan; let stand 20 minutes. Remove skewers and/or string from goose. Remove stuffing; place in serving bowl.

Yield: 8 servings

NUTRITION INFORMATION PER SERVING **Serving Size:** ⅛ of Recipe (without skin); Calories 700; Calories from Fat 250 **% Daily Value:** Total Fat 28g 43%; Saturated Fat 10g 50%; Cholesterol 200mg 67%; Sodium 1160mg 48%; Total Carbohydrate 48g 16%; Dietary Fiber 4g 16%; Sugars 16g; Protein 64g; Vitamin A 4%; Vitamin C 8%; Calcium 8%; Iron 46% **Dietary Exchanges:** 2 Starch, 8 Lean Meat, 1 Fat, 1 Other Carbohydrate, 3 Carbohydrate Choices

roasted orange-fennel halibut with dijon sauce

Prep Time: 35 minutes

sauce

½ cup fat-free or light mayonnaise

2 tablespoons finely chopped fresh parsley

1 tablespoon Dijon mustard

1 teaspoon grated orange peel

halibut

1 (1½-lb.) halibut fillet, cut into 4 pieces

2 tablespoons orange juice

2 tablespoons finely chopped fresh parsley

2 teaspoons grated orange peel

½ teaspoon fennel seed, crushed

½ teaspoon garlic salt

1. Heat oven to 425°F. Spray shallow baking pan with non-stick cooking spray. In small bowl, combine all sauce ingredients; mix well. Cover; refrigerate until serving time.

2. Place halibut in sprayed pan. Brush with orange juice. Sprinkle with 2 tablespoons parsley, 2 teaspoons orange peel, the fennel and garlic salt; rub in with fingers.

3. Bake at 425°F. for 15 to 20 minutes or until fish flakes easily with fork. Serve fish with sauce.

Yield: 4 servings

NUTRITION INFORMATION PER SERVING
Serving Size: ¼ of Recipe; Calories 170; Calories from Fat 20 **% Daily Value:** Total Fat 2g 3%; Saturated Fat 1g 5%; Cholesterol 90mg 30%; Sodium 600mg 25%; Total Carbohydrate 5g 2%; Dietary Fiber 0g 0%; Sugars 3g; Protein 32g; Vitamin A 8%; Vitamin C 6%; Calcium 2%; Iron 4% **Dietary Exchanges:** 4½ Very Lean Meat, 0 Carbohydrate Choice

deviled lobster tails

Prep Time: 45 minutes

2 teaspoons salt

4 (about 10-oz. each) frozen lobster tails

4 tablespoons butter, melted

4 green onions, sliced

2 tablespoons all-purpose flour

1½ cups half-and-half

¼ cup cocktail sauce

2 teaspoons Worcestershire sauce

1 teaspoon dry mustard

½ teaspoon salt

½ teaspoon hot pepper sauce

⅓ cup unseasoned dry bread crumbs

1. In Dutch oven, combine 2 quarts water and 2 teaspoons salt; bring to a boil. Add lobster tails; return to a boil. Cook 8 to 10 minutes or until lobster shells turn red and meat is opaque. Immediately plunge lobster tails into cold water to stop cooking. (Lobster will not be thoroughly cooked, but will continue to cook during baking step.)

2. Meanwhile, heat oven to 450°F. In medium saucepan, combine 2 tablespoons of the melted butter and the onions; cook and stir over medium heat for 2 minutes or until onions are tender. Add flour; cook and stir until mixture is smooth and bubbly. Gradually add half-and-half, stirring constantly. Bring to a boil. Cook 1 minute, stirring constantly. Add cocktail sauce, Worcestershire sauce, dry mustard, ½ teaspoon salt and the hot pepper sauce; mix well. Remove from heat.

3. With kitchens scissors, cut and remove membrane from under side of each lobster tail; discard membrane. Remove lobster meat, cut into chunks (reserve shell). Add meat to sauce; mix well. Return mixture to lobster tail shells. Place in ungreased shallow baking dish. To prevent lobster tails from tipping over, place small crumbled pieces of foil between tails.

4. In small bowl, combine remaining 2 tablespoons melted butter and the bread crumbs; mix well. Sprinkle over lobster mixture.

5. Bake at 450°F. for 10 minutes or until thoroughly heated and bread crumbs are browned.

Yield: 4 servings

NUTRITION INFORMATION PER SERVING
Serving Size: ¼ of Recipe; Calories 430; Calories from Fat 205 **% Daily Value:** Total Fat 23g 35%; Saturated Fat 14g 70%; Cholesterol 170mg 57%; Sodium 1860mg 78%; Total Carbohydrate 21g 7%; Dietary Fiber 1g 4%; Sugars 10g; Protein 35g; Vitamin A 32%; Vitamin C 4%; Calcium 22%; Iron 10% **Dietary Exchanges:** 1 Starch, 4½ Lean Meat, 2 Fat, 1½ Carbohydrate Choices

italian roasted salmon

Prep Time: 30 minutes

¼ cup purchased Italian salad dressing

2 tablespoons chopped fresh parsley

½ teaspoon dried basil leaves

1 tablespoon lemon juice

1 (1-lb.) salmon fillet

Lemon slices

1. Heat oven to 425°F. Line shallow baking pan with foil. Spray foil with nonstick cooking spray. In shallow dish, combine salad dressing, parsley, basil and lemon juice; mix well.

2. Place salmon, skin side down, in sprayed foil-lined pan. Spoon about half of salad dressing mixture over salmon.

3. Bake at 425°F. for 15 to 20 minutes or until fish flakes easily with fork, spooning remaining salad dressing mixture over fish once or twice during baking. Serve fish with lemon slices.

Yield: 4 servings

NUTRITION INFORMATION PER SERVING
Serving Size: ¼ of Recipe; Calories 225; Calories from Fat 115 **% Daily Value:** Total Fat 13g 20%; Saturated Fat 2g 10%; Cholesterol 80mg 27%; Sodium 200mg 8%; Total Carbohydrate 2g 1%; Dietary Fiber 0g 0%; Sugars 2g; Protein 25g; Vitamin A 6%; Vitamin C 4%; Calcium 4%; Iron 4% **Dietary Exchanges:** 3½ Lean Meat, ½ Fat, 0 Carbohydrate Choice

Do-Ahead
This is a great recipe to double up on so you wind up with more than you need. Leftover salmon tastes great cold and can be served on crackers or mixed in salads.

bagel 'n brie brunch strata

Prep Time: 10 minutes   (Ready in 9 hours 5 minutes)

6 eggs

1¼ cups milk

3 plain bagels, split, cut into ½-inch pieces

1 (8-oz.) round Brie cheese, rind removed, cut into ½-inch pieces

1 (16-oz.) pkg. frozen bell pepper and onion stir-fry, thawed, patted dry with paper towels

1 teaspoon dried basil leaves

½ teaspoon salt

¼ teaspoon pepper

1. Spray 13×9-inch (3-quart) glass baking dish with nonstick cooking spray. Beat eggs and milk in large bowl until well blended. Add all remaining ingredients; mix well. Pour into sprayed baking dish. Cover with foil. Refrigerate at least 8 hours or overnight.

2. To serve, heat oven to 350°F. Uncover baking dish; bake 50 to 55 minutes or until golden brown and center is set.

Yield: 8 servings

NUTRITION INFORMATION PER SERVING
Serving Size: ⅛ of Recipe; Calories 260; Calories from Fat 120 **% Daily Value:** Total Fat 13g 20%; Saturated Fat 7g 35%; Cholesterol 190mg 63%; Sodium 510mg 21%; Total Carbohydrate 18g 6%; Dietary Fiber 2g 8%; Sugars 5g; Protein 15g; Vitamin A 12%; Vitamin C 22%; Calcium 14%; Iron 8% **Dietary Exchanges:** 1 Starch, 2 Medium-Fat Meat, ½ Fat, 1 Carbohydrate Choice

Do-Ahead
This strata is great to make when you have overnight guests; it's a snap to pull together the night before and just needs to be popped in the oven the next morning. While it bakes, there's plenty of time to cut up fruit and set the table.

5 All the Trimmings

Broccoli with Walnut-Garlic Butter 140

Honey-Mustard Dilled
Brussels Sprouts 141

Almond Baby Carrots 143

Parmesan-Garlic Butter
Green Beans 145

Tarragon Green Peas 146

Sweet Potatoes with Apples
and Onions 147

Three-Potato Gratin 149

Smoky Cheese and Potato Bake 151

Potatoes Alfredo with Garden Peas 152

Garlic Smashed Red Potatoes 153

Baked Herbed Polenta Stars 154

Italian Mixed Green Salad 155

Mediterranean Fennel Salad 157

Winter Greens with Pomegranate-
Champagne Vinaigrette 158

Winter Fruit Salad 159

Jiggle Bell Salad 161

Festive Coleslaw with Citrus
Vinaigrette 162

Baked Brandied Cranberries 163

broccoli with walnut-garlic butter

Prep Time: 10 minutes

1 (14-oz.) pkg. frozen broccoli florets

1 tablespoon butter

1 garlic clove, minced

¼ cup walnut pieces

1. Cook broccoli as directed on package. Drain.

2. Meanwhile, melt butter in small saucepan over low heat. Add garlic; cook until butter is lightly browned, stirring constantly. Stir in walnuts.

3. Pour walnut mixture over cooked broccoli; toss gently to coat.

Yield: 6 (½-cup) servings

NUTRITION INFORMATION PER SERVING
Serving Size: ½ Cup; Calories 75; Calories from Fat 45 **% Daily Value:** Total Fat 5g 8%; Saturated Fat 2g 10%; Cholesterol 5mg 2%; Sodium 25mg 1%; Total Carbohydrate 4g 1%; Dietary Fiber 2g 8%; Sugars 1g; Protein 3g; Vitamin A 22%; Vitamin C 20%; Calcium 4%; Iron 2% **Dietary Exchanges:** 1 Vegetable, 1 Fat, 0 Other Carbohydrate

Family Ties
Got a crowd coming over? This recipe can be doubled for a large gathering. Microwave the broccoli in two batches; it takes the same amount of time as one large batch, and smaller amounts cook more evenly.

honey-mustard dilled brussels sprouts

Prep Time: 15 minutes

12 oz. fresh Brussels sprouts
(about 2¼ cups)

1 tablespoon butter, melted

1 tablespoon honey

1 teaspoon Dijon mustard

⅛ teaspoon onion powder

⅛ teaspoon dried dill weed

1. Trim Brussels sprouts; cut small X in stem end. Place in medium saucepan; add ½ cup water. Cover; cook over medium-high heat for 8 minutes or until tender. Drain; return to saucepan.

2. Add all remaining ingredients to cooked Brussels sprouts; toss gently to coat.

Yield: 4 (½-cup) servings

NUTRITION INFORMATION PER SERVING
Serving Size: ½ Cup; Calories 85; Calories from Fat 25 **% Daily Value:** Total Fat 3g 5%; Saturated Fat 2g 10%; Cholesterol 10mg 3%; Sodium 70mg 3%; Total Carbohydrate 11g 4%; Dietary Fiber 3g 12%; Sugars 6g; Protein 3g; Vitamin A 14%; Vitamin C 30%; Calcium 2%; Iron 4% **Dietary Exchanges:** 1 Vegetable, ½ Fat, ½ Other Carbohydrate, 1 Carbohydrate Choice

Substitution

With all the different kinds of mustards available these days, you may want to try something other than Dijon. Pick a favorite, or try something new—it's your choice.

almond baby carrots

Prep Time: 15 minutes

1 (16-oz.) pkg. fresh baby carrots

2 tablespoons slivered almonds

2 tablespoons butter

2 tablespoons amaretto

Dash salt

1 tablespoon chopped fresh parsley

1. In 1½-quart microwave-safe casserole, combine carrots and ¼ cup water; cover. Microwave on High for 7 to 10 minutes or until tender, stirring once halfway through cooking. Drain.

2. Meanwhile, cook almonds in medium saucepan over medium heat for 3 to 5 minutes or until toasted, stirring frequently.

3. Add butter, amaretto, salt and cooked carrots to saucepan; mix well. Cook 2 to 3 minutes or until most of liquid is evaporated, stirring occasionally. Sprinkle with parsley.

Yield: 6 (½-cup) servings

NUTRITION INFORMATION PER SERVING
Serving Size: ½ Cup; Calories 90; Calories from Fat 45 **% Daily Value:** Total Fat 5g 8%; Saturated Fat 3g 15%; Cholesterol 10mg 3%; Sodium 75mg 3%; Total Carbohydrate 10g 3%; Dietary Fiber 2g 8%; Sugars 6g; Protein 1g; Vitamin A 100%; Vitamin C 6%; Calcium 2%; Iron 2% **Dietary Exchanges:** 1 Vegetable, 1 Fat, ½ Carbohydrate Choice

Substitution
If you want to skip the amaretto, use 2 tablespoons of water and ⅛ teaspoon of almond extract instead.

your personal stamp

1. Adorn gift cards, wrapping paper and/or paper bags for gifts with your own stamped creations.

2. Embellish them with a touch of glitter and a flourish of ribbon to add sparkle.

parmesan-garlic
butter green beans

Prep Time: 15 minutes

1 (14-oz.) pkg. frozen whole green beans

2 tablespoons butter

1 small garlic clove, minced

1 tablespoon grated Parmesan cheese

1. Cook green beans as directed on package. Drain.

2. Meanwhile, melt butter in small saucepan over medium-low heat. Add garlic; cook 2 to 3 minutes or until garlic is tender, stirring frequently.

3. Pour garlic butter over cooked green beans; stir to coat. Sprinkle with cheese; toss gently.

Yield: 6 servings

NUTRITION INFORMATION PER SERVING
Serving Size: ⅙ of Recipe; Calories 55; Calories from Fat 35 **% Daily Value:** Total Fat 4g 6%; Saturated Fat 3g 15%; Cholesterol 10mg 3%; Sodium 50mg 2%; Total Carbohydrate 4g 1%; Dietary Fiber 1g 4%; Sugars 2g; Protein 1g; Vitamin A 10%; Vitamin C 2%; Calcium 4%; Iron 2% **Dietary Exchanges:** 1 Vegetable, 1 Fat, 0 Carbohydrate Choice

tarragon green peas

Prep Time: 15 minutes

1 (1-lb.) pkg. frozen sweet peas

3 tablespoons butter

2 green onions, sliced

⅛ teaspoon dried tarragon leaves

1. Cook peas as directed on package. Drain.

2. Meanwhile, melt butter in small saucepan over medium heat. Add onions; cook 2 to 3 minutes or until onions are tender, stirring occasionally. Stir in tarragon.

3. Pour onion-butter mixture over cooked peas; stir to coat.

Yield: 6 (½-cup) servings

Pictured on page 110.

NUTRITION INFORMATION PER SERVING
Serving Size: ½ Cup; Calories 110; Calories from Fat 55 **% Daily Value:** Total Fat 6g 9%; Saturated Fat 4g 20%; Cholesterol 15mg 5%; Sodium 95mg 4%; Total Carbohydrate 10g 3%; Dietary Fiber 3g 12%; Sugars 4g; Protein 4g; Vitamin A 12%; Vitamin C 6%; Calcium 2%; Iron 6% **Dietary Exchanges:** ½ Starch, 1½ Fat, ½ Carbohydrate Choice

Substitution

It's fine to use ½ teaspoon of chopped fresh tarragon in place of the dried tarragon if you have some on hand.

sweet potatoes with apples and onions

Prep Time: 40 minutes

1½ lb. dark-orange sweet potatoes (4 to 5 medium), peeled, cut in half lengthwise and sliced

1 tablespoon olive oil

2 cups sliced red onion (1 large)

1 Granny Smith apple, peeled, sliced

1½ cups apple juice

¼ cup firmly packed brown sugar

¼ teaspoon salt

Dash pepper

1. Place sweet potato slices in large saucepan or Dutch oven; add enough cold water to cover. Bring to a boil. Cover loosely; cook over medium heat for 9 to 13 minutes or until tender. Drain.

2. Meanwhile, heat oil in large nonstick skillet over medium-high heat until hot. Add onion; cook 2 minutes. Add all remaining ingredients; mix well. Cook 10 to 15 minutes or until mixture is reduced to a glaze, stirring occasionally.

3. Add cooked sweet potatoes to skillet; stir gently to coat. Remove from heat; let stand 1 minute before serving.

Yield: 8 (¾-cup) servings

Family Ties

Sweet potatoes can vary from pale yellow to dark orange. The dark-orange variety tends to work best in this recipe. Get the kids involved in prepping by having them peel the potatoes—just be sure the potatoes are cool enough to handle.

NUTRITION INFORMATION PER SERVING
Serving Size: ¾ Cup; Calories 160; Calories from Fat 20 **% Daily Value:** Total Fat 2g 3%; Saturated Fat 0g 0%; Cholesterol 0mg 0%; Sodium 85mg 4%; Total Carbohydrate 33g 11%; Dietary Fiber 2g 8%; Sugars 24g; Protein 2g; Vitamin A 100%; Vitamin C 16%; Calcium 2%; Iron 4% **Dietary Exchanges:** 1 Starch, ½ Fat, 1 Other Carbohydrate, 2 Carbohydrate Choices

three-potato gratin

Prep Time: 20 minutes   (Ready in 1 hour 20 minutes)

3 medium dark-orange sweet potatoes or yams (1 lb.), peeled

3 medium red-skinned potatoes (1 lb.), unpeeled

3 medium Yukon Gold potatoes (1 lb.), unpeeled

8 oz. (2 cups) finely shredded Swiss cheese

1 cup beef broth

1 teaspoon dried rosemary leaves, crushed

¼ teaspoon pepper

2 garlic cloves, minced

1. Heat oven to 400°F. Spray 12×8-inch (2-quart) glass baking dish and a sheet of foil with nonstick cooking spray. Cut all potatoes into ⅛-inch-thick slices. Layer half of potatoes in sprayed baking dish. Top with half of the Swiss cheese. Cover with remaining potatoes.

2. In medium saucepan, combine broth, rosemary, pepper and garlic. Bring to a boil. Pour boiling broth over potatoes. Loosely cover with sprayed sheet of foil. Bake at 400°F. for 45 minutes.

3. Remove baking dish from oven. Uncover dish; sprinkle with remaining half of cheese. Return to oven; bake uncovered for an additional 15 minutes or until potatoes are tender and cheese is melted.

Yield: 9 servings

NUTRITION INFORMATION PER SERVING
Serving Size: ⅑ of Recipe; Calories 240; Calories from Fat 65 **% Daily Value:** Total Fat 7g 11%; Saturated Fat 5g 25%; Cholesterol 25mg 8%; Sodium 190mg 8%; Total Carbohydrate 34g 11%; Dietary Fiber 3g 12%; Sugars 8g; Protein 10g; Vitamin A 100%; Vitamin C 18%; Calcium 26%; Iron 8% **Dietary Exchanges:** 1 Starch, 1 High-Fat Meat, 1 Other Carbohydrate, 2 Carbohydrate Choices

Do-Ahead
Make quick work of this gratin by making it ahead. Early in the day, assemble it and bake for 45 minutes. Remove it from the oven. When cool, cover and then refrigerate it. About 30 minutes before you want to serve it, uncover it, top it with the remaining cheese and bake it at 375°F. until thoroughly heated, about 30 minutes.

vellum luminaria

1. Cut one 8½×11-inch sheet of vellum lengthwise in half into two 4¼×11-inch strips.

2. Wrap each strip around glass votive candle-
   holder; glue edges.

3. Punch holes through vellum using a hole
   punch.

4. Thread ribbons through the holes and tie the
   ribbons into bows.

5. Add votive candles.

smoky cheese and potato bake

Prep Time: 10 minutes   (Ready in 6 hours 10 minutes)

1 (10¾-oz.) can condensed cream of mushroom soup

1 (8-oz.) container (about 1 cup) sour cream

1 (7-oz.) round hickory-smoked Gouda cheese, cut into ½-inch cubes

⅓ cup roasted red bell pepper strips (from a jar)

1 (32-oz.) pkg. (8 cups) frozen southern-style cubed hash-brown potatoes, thawed

1. Spray 3½- to 4-quart slow cooker with nonstick cooking spray. In medium bowl, combine soup, sour cream and cheese; mix well. Gently stir in roasted pepper strips.

2. Arrange half of potatoes in sprayed slow cooker. Top with half of sour cream mixture; spread evenly. Top with remaining potatoes and sour cream mixture, spreading evenly. Do not stir.

3. Cover; cook on Low setting for 5 to 6 hours.

Yield: 14 (½-cup) servings

NUTRITION INFORMATION PER SERVING
Serving Size: ½ Cup; Calories 180; Calories from Fat 70 **% Daily Value:** Total Fat 8g 12%; Saturated Fat 5g 25%; Cholesterol 30mg 10%; Sodium 300mg 13%; Total Carbohydrate 21g 7%; Dietary Fiber 1g 4%; Sugars 2g; Protein 6g; Vitamin A 8%; Vitamin C 10%; Calcium 12%; Iron 2% **Dietary Exchanges:** 1 Starch, ½ High-Fat Meat, ½ Fat, ½ Other Carbohydrate, 1½ Carbohydrate Choices

Substitution

Condensed cream of celery soup will work in place of the cream of mushroom soup. You may also want to experiment with different kinds of cheese as well.

potatoes alfredo with garden peas

Prep Time: 10 minutes   (Ready in 4 hours 40 minutes)

2 lb. small (2- to 3-inch) red potatoes, cut into ¼-inch-thick slices (8 cups)

¼ cup sliced green onions

2 garlic cloves, minced

1 (10-oz.) container refrigerated Alfredo sauce

½ cup half-and-half or milk

½ teaspoon salt

⅛ teaspoon pepper

1½ cups frozen sweet peas (from 1-lb. pkg.)

1. Spray 3½- to 4-quart slow cooker with nonstick cooking spray. Layer half each of potatoes, onions and garlic in sprayed slow cooker.

2. In medium bowl, combine Alfredo sauce, half-and-half, salt and pepper; mix well. Spoon half of mixture over top of potato mixture. Layer with remaining potatoes, onions, garlic and sauce mixture. Do not stir.

3. Cover; cook on High setting for 3 to 4 hours.

4. About 30 minutes before serving, sprinkle peas over potato mixture. Cover; cook on High setting an additional 20 to 30 minutes. Stir gently to mix peas with potatoes before serving.

Yield: 10 (½-cup) servings

NUTRITION INFORMATION PER SERVING
Serving Size: ½ Cup; Calories 210; Calories from Fat 100 **% Daily Value:** Total Fat 11g 17%; Saturated Fat 7g 35%; Cholesterol 30mg 10%; Sodium 270mg 11%; Total Carbohydrate 24g 8%; Dietary Fiber 2g 8%; Sugars 3g; Protein 5g; Vitamin A 10%; Vitamin C 10%; Calcium 10%; Iron 8% **Dietary Exchanges:** 1½ Starch, 2 Fat, 1½ Carbohydrate Choices

Special Touch

For added flavor, toss 1 teaspoon dried dill weed into the slow cooker when you add the peas. It will complement the potatoes as well as the green peas.

garlic smashed red potatoes

Prep Time: 15 minutes   (Ready in 4 hours 45 minutes)

3 lb. small (2- to 3-inch) red potatoes

4 garlic cloves, minced

2 tablespoons olive oil

1 teaspoon salt

½ cup water

½ cup chive and onion cream cheese spread (from 8-oz. container)

¼ to ½ cup milk

1. Halve or quarter potatoes as necessary to make similar-sized pieces. Place in 4- to 6-quart slow cooker. Add garlic, oil, salt and water; mix well to coat all potato pieces.

2. Cover; cook on High setting for 3½ to 4½ hours or until potatoes are tender.

3. With fork or potato masher, mash potatoes and garlic. Add cream cheese; stir until well blended. Stir in enough milk for soft serving consistency. Serve immediately, or cover and hold in slow cooker on Low setting for up to 2 hours.

Yield: 14 (½-cup) servings

NUTRITION INFORMATION PER SERVING
Serving Size: ½ Cup; Calories 135; Calories from Fat 45 **% Daily Value:** Total Fat 5g 8%; Saturated Fat 2g 10%; Cholesterol 10mg 3%; Sodium 200mg 8%; Total Carbohydrate 20g 7%; Dietary Fiber 1g 4%; Sugars 1g; Protein 3g; Vitamin A 2%; Vitamin C 8%; Calcium 2%; Iron 6% **Dietary Exchanges:** 1 Starch, 1 Fat, 1 Carbohydrate Choice

baked herbed polenta stars

Prep Time: 15 minutes   (Ready in 1 hour)

1½ teaspoons salt

1½ cups yellow cornmeal

½ cup whipping cream

¼ cup grated Parmesan cheese

2 teaspoons dried Italian seasoning

1 tablespoon olive oil

1. Grease 15×10×1-inch baking pan. In large saucepan, bring 5 cups water and salt to a boil. While stirring water in a circular motion with wire whisk, add cornmeal in a slow steady stream, keeping water boiling continuously. Reduce heat to low; continue cooking, stirring constantly, until mixture is thick, 5 to 15 minutes depending on type of cornmeal.

2. Add cream, cheese and Italian seasoning; mix well. Pour into greased pan. Cool 15 minutes. At this point, polenta can be covered and refrigerated until serving time.

3. To serve, heat oven to 400°F. With assorted star-shaped cookie cutters, cut polenta into stars. (Polenta scraps can be combined and rerolled to cut additional stars.) Brush both sides of each star with oil; place on ungreased cookie sheets.

4. Bake at 400°F. for 10 to 15 minutes or until thoroughly heated.

Yield: 10 servings

NUTRITION INFORMATION PER SERVING
Serving Size: 1/10 of Recipe; Calories 135; Calories from Fat 55 **% Daily Value: Total Fat** 6g 9%; Saturated Fat 3g 15%; Cholesterol 15mg 5%; Sodium 410mg 17%; Total Carbohydrate 17g 6%; Dietary Fiber 1g 4%; Sugars 2g; Protein 3g; Vitamin A 4%; Vitamin C 0%; Calcium 4%; Iron 6% **Dietary Exchanges:** 1 Starch, 1 Fat, 1 Carbohydrate Choice

Family Ties
These polenta stars are particularly pretty when they are cut in different sizes. Purchase several sizes or a graduated set of star cookie cutters from a cookware store and get the whole family involved in cutting out shapes.

italian mixed green salad

Prep Time: 20 minutes

9 cups torn mixed salad greens (such as romaine, iceberg, leaf or Bibb lettuce, arugula, escarole and/or curly endive)

3 medium tomatoes, cut into wedges

½ large red onion, cut in half, thinly sliced

2 green bell peppers, cut into thin bite-sized strips

½ cup chopped fresh parsley

2 tablespoons chopped fresh basil

½ teaspoon salt

½ cup olive or vegetable oil

⅓ cup red or white wine vinegar

1. In large bowl, combine salad greens, tomatoes, onion and bell peppers. Sprinkle with parsley, basil and salt.

2. Just before serving, drizzle salad with oil and vinegar; toss until well coated.

Yield: 12 (1-cup) servings

Pictured on page 110.

NUTRITION INFORMATION PER SERVING
Serving Size: 1 Cup; Calories 105; Calories from Fat 80 **% Daily Value:** Total Fat 9g 14%; Saturated Fat 1g 5%; Cholesterol 0mg 0%; Sodium 115mg 5%; Total Carbohydrate 5g 2%; Dietary Fiber 1g 4%; Sugars 2g; Protein 1g; Vitamin A 36%; Vitamin C 28%; Calcium 2%; Iron 6% **Dietary Exchanges:** 1 Vegetable, 2 Fat, 1 Carbohydrate Choice

Substitution
Make the most of your time by replacing the 9 cups of torn mixed salad greens with an equal amount of baby spring greens. Buy them prepackaged or in bulk from your grocer's produce department.

mediterranean fennel salad

2 (14-oz.) pkg. frozen whole green beans

2 bulbs fresh fennel

2 medium red bell peppers, cut into bite-sized strips

3 tablespoons red wine vinegar

1 tablespoon Dijon mustard

1 teaspoon minced garlic

½ teaspoon salt

½ cup extra-virgin olive oil

¼ cup pine nuts

1. Cook green beans as directed on package. Drain; rinse with cold water to cool.

2. Trim fennel bulbs; cut in half. Cut each half into ¼-inch-thick slices. In large bowl, combine fennel, bell peppers and cooked green beans.

3. In small bowl, combine vinegar and mustard; beat with wire whisk until well blended. On cutting board, mash garlic and salt together with fork to make a paste. Beat into vinegar mixture. Slowly beat in oil until well blended.

4. Add dressing to vegetable mixture; toss gently to mix. Arrange on large serving platter. Sprinkle with pine nuts. If desired, garnish with fresh fennel tops.

Yield: 10 (1¼-cup) servings

NUTRITION INFORMATION PER SERVING
Serving Size: 1¼ Cups; Calories 170; Calories from Fat 115 **% Daily Value: Total Fat** 13g 20%; Saturated Fat 2g 10%; Cholesterol 0mg 0%; Sodium 190mg 8%; Total Carbohydrate 11g 4%; Dietary Fiber 4g 16%; Sugars 4g; Protein 2g; Vitamin A 38%; Vitamin C 44%; Calcium 6%; Iron 6% **Dietary Exchanges:** 2 Vegetable, 2½ Fat, 1 Carbohydrate Choice

Special Touch

All olive oils are not created equal. Extra-virgin olive oil is extracted from the first pressing of olives, using a chemical-free, cold-pressing process. This procedure produces a very flavorful oil with the lowest level of acid content. Extra-virgin olive oil is a great choice for dressing salads, where its pure flavor can be appreciated.

winter greens with pomegranate-champagne vinaigrette

Prep Time: 20 minutes

2 (10-oz.) pkg. mixed salad greens

1 pomegranate

¼ cup champagne wine vinegar

1 tablespoon Dijon mustard

¾ cup vegetable oil

¼ teaspoon salt

Dash freshly ground black pepper

1. Place greens in large salad bowl. Peel and seed pomegranate, reserving seeds.

2. In small bowl, combine vinegar and mustard; blend well. With wire whisk, slowly beat in oil until thick. Add salt and pepper. Stir in half of the pomegranate seeds.

3. Just before serving, add dressing to greens; toss to coat. Scatter remaining pomegranate seeds over salad.

Yield: 12 to 16 servings

NUTRITION INFORMATION PER SERVING
Serving Size: ⅟₁₆ of Recipe; Calories 105; Calories from Fat 90 **% Daily Value:** Total Fat 10g 15%; Saturated Fat 1g 5%; Cholesterol 0mg 0%; Sodium 70mg 3%; Total Carbohydrate 3g 1%; Dietary Fiber 0g 0%; Sugars 2g; Protein 1g; Vitamin A 22%; Vitamin C 10%; Calcium 2%; Iron 2% **Dietary Exchanges:** 2 Fat, 0 Carbohydrate Choice

Substitution

White wine vinegar can be used in place of the champagne vinegar if you like. Remember to dress the salad greens just before serving so the greens don't wilt.

winter fruit salad

Prep Time: 15 minutes

2 cups cubed unpeeled red apples (2 medium)

2 cups cubed unpeeled pears (2 medium)

¾ cup chopped dates

1 tablespoon fresh lemon juice

2 medium bananas, sliced

⅓ cup light mayonnaise or salad dressing

2 tablespoons honey

½ teaspoon grated lemon peel

⅛ teaspoon allspice

1. In large bowl, combine apples, pears, dates and lemon juice; mix well. Add bananas; stir gently to mix.

2. In small bowl, combine all remaining ingredients; blend well. Add to salad; stir gently to coat. If desired, serve in lettuce-lined bowl.

Yield: 12 (½-cup) servings

NUTRITION INFORMATION PER SERVING
Serving Size: ½ Cup; Calories 125; Calories from Fat 25 **% Daily Value:** Total Fat 3g 5%; Saturated Fat 0g 0%; Cholesterol 5mg 2%; Sodium 40mg 2%; Total Carbohydrate 24g 8%; Dietary Fiber 2g 8%; Sugars 19g; Protein 1g; Vitamin A 0%; Vitamin C 8%; Calcium 0%; Iron 2% **Dietary Exchanges:** 1 Fruit, ½ Fat, ½ Other Carbohydrate, 1½ Carbohydrate Choices

Family Ties

Crisp apples such as Braeburn and Gala are best bets for this tangy fruit salad. Feel free to mix and match the fruit, depending on what your family likes.

jiggle bell salad

Prep Time: 10 minutes   (Ready in 5 hours 5 minutes)

1½ cups cranberry-apple juice drink

2 (3-oz.) pkg. cherry flavor gelatin

2 cups sparkling water, chilled

1 (15-oz.) can mandarin orange segments, drained

Lettuce leaves

1. Oil 7-cup mold or 8 (½-cup) molds. In medium saucepan, bring cranberry-apple juice drink to a boil. Remove from heat. Add gelatin; stir until dissolved. Refrigerate 15 minutes.

2. Stir sparkling water into gelatin mixture. Refrigerate 40 minutes.

3. Fold orange segments into gelatin. Spoon into oiled mold. Refrigerate 4 hours or until firm.

4. To serve, line serving platter with lettuce. Unmold salad onto lettuce-lined platter. Cut salad into wedges to serve.

Yield: 8 servings

NUTRITION INFORMATION PER SERVING
Serving Size: ⅛ of Recipe; Calories 135; Calories from Fat 0 **% Daily Value:** Total Fat 0g 0%; Saturated Fat 0g 0%; Cholesterol 0mg 0%; Sodium 55mg 2%; Total Carbohydrate 32g 11%; Dietary Fiber 0g 0%; Sugars 30g; Protein 2g; Vitamin A 4%; Vitamin C 22%; Calcium 0%; Iron 0% **Dietary Exchanges:** ½ Fruit, 1½ Other Carbohydrates, 2 Carbohydrate Choices

Special Touch
Kids will get a kick out of this refreshing and fruity gelatin salad. For an extra dose of color, garnish with star fruit, champagne grapes and figs.

festive coleslaw with citrus vinaigrette

Prep Time: 10 minutes

1 (16-oz.) pkg. coleslaw blend

½ medium green bell pepper, cut into small thin strips

½ medium red bell pepper, cut into small thin strips

⅓ cup sugar

¼ cup orange juice

2 tablespoons lemon juice

½ teaspoon salt

½ teaspoon onion powder

½ teaspoon dry mustard

⅓ cup oil

1. In large bowl, combine coleslaw blend and bell peppers.

2. In medium bowl, combine all remaining ingredients except oil; mix well with wire whisk. Gradually beat in oil until well combined. Pour dressing over salad; mix well.

Yield: 12 (½-cup) servings

Do-Ahead
Mix the cabbage and bell peppers ahead; cover and refrigerate them for up to two hours. Prepare the vinaigrette ahead; cover and refrigerate it for up to a day. To make crisp coleslaw, combine the cabbage with the vinaigrette just before serving. If you prefer your coleslaw less crisp, mix the salad a few hours in advance, then cover and refrigerate it until serving time.

NUTRITION INFORMATION PER SERVING
Serving Size: ½ Cup; Calories 150; Calories from Fat 110 **% Daily Value:** Total Fat 12g 18%; Saturated Fat 2g 10%; Cholesterol 0mg 0%; Sodium 105mg 4%; Total Carbohydrate 9g 3%; Dietary Fiber 1g 4%; Sugars 7g; Protein 1g; Vitamin A 2%; Vitamin C 38%; Calcium 2%; Iron 2% **Dietary Exchanges:** 2½ Fat, ½ Other Carbohydrate, ½ Carbohydrate Choice

baked brandied cranberries

Prep Time: 5 minutes   (Ready in 1 hour 5 minutes)

1 (12-oz.) pkg. fresh cranberries

1½ cups sugar

2 teaspoons grated orange peel

3 tablespoons brandy

1. Heat oven to 350°F. In 1½-quart casserole, combine all ingredients; mix well. Cover.

2. Bake at 350°F. for 20 minutes. Uncover casserole; stir mixture. Bake uncovered an additional 30 to 40 minutes or until cranberries pop and mixture is slightly thickened. Serve warm or cold.

Yield: 8 (¼-cup) servings

NUTRITION INFORMATION PER SERVING
Serving Size: ¼ Cup; Calories 170; Calories from Fat 0 **% Daily Value:** Total Fat 0g 0%; Saturated Fat 0g 0%; Cholesterol 0mg 0%; Sodium 0mg 0%; Total Carbohydrate 43g 14%; Dietary Fiber 1g 4%; Sugars 40g; Protein 0g; Vitamin A 0%; Vitamin C 4%; Calcium 0%; Iron 0% **Dietary Exchanges:** 1 Fruit, 2 Other Carbohydrates, 3 Carbohydrate Choices

Substitution
You can use frozen cranberries to make this tangy-sweet cranberry relish if you like; just add 5 to 10 minutes to the baking time. Either way, it tastes great when paired with a pork, ham, chicken or turkey main dish.

6 *Delectable Desserts*

Chocolate-Almond Mousse Cake 166

Christmas Angel Cake 168

Quick Saucy Cranberry Cake 171

Dark Gingerbread Bundt Cake 172

Holiday Cherry-Chocolate Cake 173

Cranberry-Apple Streusel Pie 175

Chocolate-Cashew Pie 176

Strawberry-Fudge Pie 177

Triple-Chocolate Truffle Trees 179

Individual Lemon-Lime Cream Tarts 180

Pomegranate Tartlets 181

Orange Crème Dessert with Ruby
Cranberry Sauce 182

Eggnog Ice Cream Dessert 184

Raspberry Cream Heart 185

Chocolate-Cherry Cheesecake 187

Spiced Cider Cheesecake 188

Mocha Truffle Cheesecake 190

Cranberry-Peach Gingerbread Trifle 192

Eggnog Bread Pudding
with Cherry-Bourbon Sauce 193

Creamy Peppermint-Topped
Brownie Dessert 195

Caffé Latte Crème Brûlée 196

Cranberry Mousse 197

chocolate-almond mousse cake

Prep Time: 50 minutes   (Ready in 1 hour 10 minutes)

cake

1 (1 lb. 2.25-oz.) pkg. devil's food cake mix with pudding

1⅓ cups water

½ cup vegetable oil

3 eggs

mousse

12 oz. semisweet chocolate, cut into pieces

½ cup whipping cream

¼ teaspoon almond extract

2½ cups whipping cream, whipped

topping

2 tablespoons sliced almonds, toasted

1. Heat oven to 350°F. Spray 15×10×1-inch baking pan with nonstick cooking spray. Line bottom with waxed paper; spray paper. Prepare cake mix as directed on package using water, oil and eggs. Pour batter into sprayed paper-lined pan.

2. Bake at 350°F. for 18 to 20 minutes or until cake springs back when touched lightly in center. Cool cake in pan on wire rack for 10 minutes. Invert cake onto wire rack; remove pan and paper. Cool 15 minutes or until completely cooled.

3. Meanwhile, melt chocolate and ½ cup whipping cream in medium saucepan over low heat, stirring constantly. Remove from heat. Stir in almond extract. Cool 10 minutes or until slightly cooled. Fold cooled chocolate mixture into whipped cream.

4. Trim edges of cake. Cut cake lengthwise into 2 long layers. Place 1 layer on serving platter. Spread with ⅓ of mousse. Repeat with remaining cake layer and ⅓ of mousse. Place remaining ⅓ of mousse in decorating bag fitted with star tip. Pipe border around bottom and top of cake. Decorate top of cake with mousse rosettes. Sprinkle almonds over top. Store in refrigerator.

Yield: 16 servings

Do-Ahead

Bake the cake in advance and let it cool. Cut it as directed in the recipe, then wrap it tightly with plastic wrap and foil. Seal it in a plastic food-storage freezer bag and freeze it for up to three days. The mousse can be made one day in advance. Assemble the frozen cake with the chilled mousse early in the day; cover and refrigerate. Remove from the refrigerator one hour before serving.

NUTRITION INFORMATION PER SERVING
Serving Size: ¹⁄₁₆ of Recipe; Calories 460; Calories from Fat 280 **% Daily Value:** Total Fat 31g 48%; Saturated Fat 14g 70%; Cholesterol 90mg 30%; Sodium 320mg 13%; Total Carbohydrate 40g 13%; Dietary Fiber 2g 8%; Sugars 30g; Protein 5g; Vitamin A 10%; Vitamin C 0%; Calcium 8%; Iron 10% **Dietary Exchanges:** 1½ Starch, 6 Fat, 1 Other Carbohydrate, 2½ Carbohydrate Choices

christmas angel cake

Prep Time: 1 hour   (Ready in 2 hours 15 minutes)

cake

1 (1 lb. 2.25-oz.) pkg. white cake mix with pudding

1¼ cups water

⅓ cup vegetable oil

3 egg whites

frosting and decorations

1 foil baking cup

1 (16-oz.) can vanilla ready-to-spread frosting

2 cups frozen whipped topping, thawed

¼ cup flaked coconut

Edible glitter

Small candies

Yellow food color

1 wafer cookie

1. Heat oven to 350°F. Spray bottom only of 13×9-inch pan with nonstick cooking spray. Line bottom of pan with waxed paper; spray and lightly flour paper. Generously spray and flour 10-oz. custard cup.

2. Prepare cake mix as directed on package using water, oil and egg whites. Pour ½ cup batter into sprayed and floured custard cup. Pour remaining batter evenly into sprayed and floured paper-lined pan.

3. Bake at 350°F. until cake springs back when touched lightly in center. Bake custard cup for 20 to 30 minutes; bake 13×9-inch pan for 28 to 33 minutes. Cool cakes in cup and pan on wire rack for 15 minutes. Invert cakes onto wire rack; remove cup, pan and paper. Cool 30 minutes or until completely cooled.

4. Invert large cake onto flat serving tray or foil-covered 20×15-inch cardboard. To form angel shape, starting at center of one short side, make 2 diagonal cuts to corners of opposite short side, forming a triangular piece in center. (See diagram A.) Separate pieces 1 and 2 from piece 3 at bottom of cake to form wings. (See diagram B.)

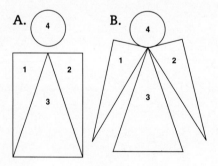

5. For angel's halo and head, flatten foil baking cup; place at point of center triangle between wings. Invert small round cake onto halo.

6. In medium bowl, combine frosting and whipped topping; blend well. Reserve ¼ cup frosting mixture for hair. Frost sides and tops of cake pieces. Sprinkle coconut over wings. Sprinkle wings with edible glitter.

7. Place small candies on cake for eyes, mouth and buttons. Add yellow food color to reserved frosting mixture; blend well. Spread or pipe yellow frosting on head for hair. Cut wafer cookie; add to cake for songbook. Attach small candies with frosting for hands. Store in refrigerator.

Yield: 10 servings

a place for everyone

1. Attach a miniature ornament and a sprig of greenery or an herb to the napkin at each place setting.

2. Personalize the ornament with the guest's name or add a small name tag.

quick saucy cranberry cake

Prep Time: 15 minutes   (Ready in 1 hour 25 minutes)

1 (15.6-oz.) pkg. cranberry-orange quick bread mix

½ cup water

2 tablespoons vegetable oil

2 eggs

1 cup fresh cranberries

¾ cup firmly packed brown sugar

1¼ cups boiling water

1. Heat oven to 350°F. Spray 8-inch square (2-quart) glass baking dish with nonstick cooking spray. In large bowl, combine bread mix, water, oil and eggs; stir 50 to 75 strokes with spoon until mix is moistened.

2. Sprinkle cranberries in sprayed baking dish. Spoon and spread batter evenly over cranberries. Sprinkle with brown sugar. Pour boiling water evenly over batter.

3. Bake at 350°F. for 35 to 40 minutes or until cake is golden brown and top springs back when touched lightly in center. Cool at least 30 minutes.

4. To serve, cut cake into squares; invert squares onto individual dessert plates. If desired, top with sweetened whipped cream. Store in refrigerator.

Yield: 9 servings

NUTRITION INFORMATION PER SERVING
Serving Size: ⅑ of Recipe; Calories 320; Calories from Fat 70 **% Daily Value:** Total Fat 8g 12%; Saturated Fat 1g 5%; Cholesterol 45mg 15%; Sodium 250mg 10%; Total Carbohydrate 58g 19%; Dietary Fiber 0g 0%; Sugars 40g; Protein 4g; Vitamin A 0%; Vitamin C 0%; Calcium 2%; Iron 4% **Dietary Exchanges:** 1 Starch, 1½ Fat, 3 Other Carbohydrates, 4 Carbohydrate Choices

Substitution
Frozen cranberries can be used in this recipe in place of the fresh ones; just thaw them before using. The holiday season is a great time to pick up a couple extra bags of fresh cranberries. Toss them in the freezer and keep them for future winter baking projects as they arise.

dark gingerbread bundt cake

Prep Time: 15 minutes   (Ready in 2 hours 15 minutes)

2½ cups all-purpose flour

1 cup sugar

¼ cup unsweetened cocoa

2 teaspoons ground ginger

1½ teaspoons baking powder

¾ teaspoon baking soda

½ teaspoon salt

½ teaspoon cinnamon

½ teaspoon nutmeg

½ teaspoon cloves

2 eggs

1 cup molasses

⅓ cup vegetable oil

1 cup water

Powdered sugar, if desired

1. Heat oven to 350°F. Spray 12-cup bundt cake pan with nonstick cooking spray; lightly flour. In large bowl, combine flour, sugar, cocoa, ginger, baking powder, baking soda, salt, cinnamon, nutmeg and cloves; mix well.

2. Lightly beat eggs in medium bowl. Add molasses and oil; beat well. Stir in water. Add egg mixture to flour mixture; beat just until combined. Pour batter into sprayed and floured pan.

3. Bake at 350°F. for 45 to 60 minutes or until toothpick inserted in center comes out clean. Cool in pan on wire rack for 15 minutes. Invert cake onto serving plate; remove pan. Cool 30 minutes or until completely cooled. Just before serving, sprinkle cake with powdered sugar.

Yield: 16 servings

NUTRITION INFORMATION PER SERVING
Serving Size: ¹⁄₁₆ of Recipe; Calories 275; Calories from Fat 90 **% Daily Value:** Total Fat 10g 15%; Saturated Fat 2g 10%; Cholesterol 25mg 8%; Sodium 200mg 8%; Total Carbohydrate 43g 14%; Dietary Fiber 1g 4%; Sugars 25g; Protein 3g; Vitamin A 0%; Vitamin C 0%; Calcium 8%; Iron 12% **Dietary Exchanges:** 1 Starch, 2 Fat, 2 Other Carbohydrates, 3 Carbohydrate Choices

Special Touch
Take this cake to a special holiday party. Serve each slice with a generous dollop of sweetened whipped cream.

holiday cherry-chocolate cake

Prep Time: 35 minutes   (Ready in 55 minutes)

cake

1 (1 lb. 2.25-oz.) pkg. devil's food cake mix with pudding

2 tablespoons all-purpose flour

1¾ cups water

¾ cup refrigerated or frozen fat-free egg product, thawed, or 3 eggs

filling and topping

1 (21-oz.) can cherry pie filling

¾ teaspoon almond extract

1 (8-oz.) container frozen light whipped topping, thawed

1. Heat oven to 350°F. Spray 15×10×1-inch baking pan with nonstick cooking spray. Line bottom of pan with waxed paper; spray paper. Prepare cake mix as directed on package using flour, water and egg product. Pour batter into sprayed paper-lined pan.

2. Bake at 350°F. for 18 to 20 minutes or until cake springs back when touched lightly in center. Cool cake in pan on wire rack for 10 minutes. Invert cake onto wire rack; remove pan and paper. Cool 15 minutes or until completely cooled.

3. In small bowl, combine pie filling and ½ teaspoon of the almond extract; mix well.

4. Cut cake in half crosswise to form two 10×7-inch layers. Place 1 cake layer on serving platter or tray; spread pie filling mixture over top. Top with remaining cake layer.

5. Stir remaining ¼ teaspoon almond extract into whipped topping. Spread mixture over top and sides of cake. Serve immediately or refrigerate until serving time. Store in refrigerator.

Yield: 12 servings

NUTRITION INFORMATION PER SERVING
Serving Size: ½₂ of Recipe; Calories 290; Calories from Fat 65 **% Daily Value:** Total Fat 7g 11%; Saturated Fat 3g 15%; Cholesterol 0mg 0%; Sodium 430mg 18%; Total Carbohydrate 52g 17%; Dietary Fiber 2g 8%; Sugars 37g; Protein 5g; Vitamin A 4%; Vitamin C 2%; Calcium 8%; Iron 10% **Dietary Exchanges:** 1½ Starch, 1 Fat, 2 Other Carbohydrates, 3½ Carbohydrate Choices

Special Touch

If desired, garnish each serving with a maraschino or candied cherry and chocolate curls. Use a vegetable peeler to shave a room-temperature chocolate bar into curls. Try dark, milk or white chocolate, or go for it and try a combo.

cranberry-apple streusel pie

Prep Time: 15 minutes   (Ready in 1 hour 30 minutes)

1 refrigerated pie crust (from 15-oz. pkg.), softened as directed on package

2 (21-oz.) cans apple pie filling

1 cup sweetened dried cranberries

½ teaspoon cinnamon

⅓ cup all-purpose flour

¼ cup firmly packed brown sugar

3 tablespoons butter

1. Heat oven to 450°F. Prepare and bake pie crust as directed on package for *one-crust baked shell* using 9-inch glass pie pan. DO NOT PRICK CRUST. Reduce oven temperature to 400°F.

2. Meanwhile, in medium bowl, combine pie filling, cranberries and cinnamon; mix well.

3. In small bowl, combine flour and brown sugar; mix well. With pastry blender or fork, cut in butter until mixture resembles coarse crumbs.

4. Spoon pie filling mixture into warm baked shell. Sprinkle crumb mixture evenly over filling.

5. Bake at 400°F. for 35 to 45 minutes or until topping is golden brown and filling bubbles. If necessary, cover edge of crust with strips of foil after 5 to 10 minutes of baking to prevent excessive browning. Cool at least 30 minutes before serving.

Yield: 8 servings

NUTRITION INFORMATION PER SERVING
Serving Size: ⅛ of Recipe; Calories 430; Calories from Fat 110 **% Daily Value:** Total Fat 12g 18%; Saturated Fat 6g 30%; Cholesterol 15mg 5%; Sodium 150mg 6%; Total Carbohydrate 78g 26%; Dietary Fiber 2g 8%; Sugars 52g; Protein 2g; Vitamin A 4%; Vitamin C 2%; Calcium 2%; Iron 4% **Dietary Exchanges:** 2½ Fat, 5 Other Carbohydrates, 5 Carbohydrate Choices

Substitution
Pair another fruit pie filling with the cranberry. Instead of apple, you may want to try peach, cherry or blueberry. Whatever combo you choose, this pie is irresistible with a scoop of vanilla ice cream.

chocolate-cashew pie

Prep Time: 25 minutes   (Ready in 3 hours 45 minutes)

crust

1 refrigerated pie crust (from 15-oz. pkg.), softened as directed on package

filling and topping

¾ cup light corn syrup

½ cup sugar

3 tablespoons butter, melted

1 teaspoon vanilla

3 eggs

1 (6-oz.) pkg. (1 cup) semisweet chocolate chips

1 cup cashew halves

10 whole cashews

Whipped cream, if desired

1. Place pie crust in 9-inch glass pie pan as directed on package for *one-crust filled pie.*

2. Heat oven to 325°F. In large bowl, combine corn syrup, sugar, butter, vanilla and eggs; beat with wire whisk until well blended. Reserve 2 tablespoons chocolate chips for topping. Stir remaining chocolate chips and cashew halves into corn syrup mixture. Spread evenly in crust-lined pan.

3. Bake at 325°F. for 45 to 55 minutes or until pie is deep golden brown and filling is set. Cover edge of crust with strips of foil after 15 to 20 minutes of baking to prevent excessive browning. Cool 2½ hours or until completely cooled.

4. Meanwhile, line cookie sheet with waxed paper. Place reserved 2 tablespoons chocolate chips in small microwave-safe bowl. Microwave on High for 45 to 60 seconds or until stirred smooth. Dip each whole cashew in chocolate; place on paper-lined cookie sheet. Refrigerate 15 to 20 minutes or until chocolate is set.

5. Just before serving, garnish pie with whipped cream and chocolate-dipped cashews. Store in refrigerator.

Yield: 10 servings

NUTRITION INFORMATION PER SERVING
Serving Size: ¹/₁₀ of Recipe; Calories 445; Calories from Fat 205 **% Daily Value:** Total Fat 23g 35%; Saturated Fat 9g 45%; Cholesterol 75mg 25%; Sodium 250mg 10%; Total Carbohydrate 54g 18%; Dietary Fiber 1g 4%; Sugars 30g; Protein 6g; Vitamin A 4%; Vitamin C 0%; Calcium 2%; Iron 6% **Dietary Exchanges:** 2 Starch, 4½ Fat, 1½ Other Carbohydrates, 3½ Carbohydrate Choices

Substitution
If you're nuts for almonds, use toasted slivered almonds in place of the cashews and stir 1 tablespoon of amaretto into the filling. Garnish with whole blanched almonds dipped in melted chocolate.

strawberry-fudge pie

Prep Time: 30 minutes   (Ready in 3 hours 20 minutes)

crust

1 refrigerated pie crust (from 15-oz. pkg.), softened as directed on package

brownie layer

1 (10.25-oz.) pkg. fudge brownie mix

¼ cup vegetable oil

2 tablespoons water

1 egg

cheesecake layer

1 (8-oz.) pkg. cream cheese, softened

¼ cup sugar

1 teaspoon vanilla

1 egg

topping

3 cups fresh strawberries, halved

2 tablespoons hot fudge ice cream topping

1. Heat oven to 350°F. Place pie crust in 9-inch glass pie pan as directed on package for *one-crust filled pie.*

2. In large bowl, combine all brownie layer ingredients; beat 50 strokes with spoon. Spread in bottom of crust-lined pan.

3. Bake at 350°F. for 30 to 35 minutes or until top is shiny and center is set. If necessary, cover edge of crust with strips of foil after 15 to 20 minutes of baking to prevent excessive browning.

4. Meanwhile, in small bowl, combine all cheesecake layer ingredients; beat until smooth.

5. Remove partially baked pie from oven. Working quickly, drop cream cheese mixture by small spoonfuls over brownie layer; carefully spread to cover completely. Return to oven; bake an additional 18 to 20 minutes or until cheesecake layer is set. Cool at least 1 hour.

6. Arrange strawberry halves, cut side down, over top of cheesecake layer. Refrigerate 1 hour or until serving time.

7. Just before serving, place ice cream topping in small microwave-safe bowl. Microwave on Defrost for 45 seconds. Spoon into small resealable plastic bag; seal bag. Cut small hole in bottom corner of bag; squeeze bag to drizzle topping over pie. Store in refrigerator.

Yield: 8 servings

NUTRITION INFORMATION PER SERVING
Serving Size: ⅛ of Recipe; Calories 510; Calories from Fat 250 **% Daily Value:** Total Fat 28g 43%; Saturated Fat 11g 55%; Cholesterol 90mg 30%; Sodium 350mg 15%; Total Carbohydrate 57g 19%; Dietary Fiber 1g 4%; Sugars 35g; Protein 7g; Vitamin A 10%; Vitamin C 24%; Calcium 6%; Iron 12% **Dietary Exchanges:** 2 Starch, ½ Fruit, 5½ Fat, 1½ Other Carbohydrates, 4 Carbohydrate Choices

triple-chocolate truffle trees

Prep Time: 1 hour   (Ready in 4 hours)

crust

1 cup chocolate cookie crumbs

¼ cup sugar

¼ cup butter, melted

white chocolate layer

1 (6-oz.) pkg. white chocolate baking bar

3 tablespoons whipping cream

1 tablespoon Grand Marnier liqueur or orange juice

1 tablespoon butter

dark chocolate layer

¾ cup whipping cream

1 tablespoon butter

12 oz. semisweet chocolate, chopped

2 tablespoons Grand Marnier liqueur or orange juice

garnish

8 chocolate sticks or chocolate-coated candy sticks, broken into 1½-inch pieces

1. Heat oven to 350°F. Lightly spray 9-inch tart pan with removable bottom with nonstick cooking spray. In medium bowl, combine cookie crumbs and ¼ cup sugar; mix well. Stir in ¼ cup butter. Press crumb mixture in bottom of sprayed pan.

2. Bake at 350°F. for 10 minutes. Cool in pan on wire rack while preparing white chocolate layer.

3. Cut 1 square of white chocolate baking bar in half; reserve half. Finely chop other half of square and remaining baking bar. Set aside. In small saucepan, combine all remaining white chocolate layer ingredients; cook over medium-low heat until butter is melted and mixture is simmering, stirring occasionally. Remove from heat. Stir in chopped white chocolate until smooth. Spoon into crust-lined pan; spread gently. Refrigerate while preparing dark chocolate layer.

4. In medium saucepan, combine ¾ cup whipping cream and 1 tablespoon butter; cook over medium-low heat until butter is melted and mixture is simmering, stirring occasionally. Remove from heat. Stir in semisweet chocolate until smooth. Stir in 2 tablespoons liqueur. Spoon over white chocolate layer; spread gently. Refrigerate about 2 hours or until set.

5. About 1 hour before serving, grate reserved half square of white chocolate over surface of tart. Remove side of pan; let tart stand at room temperature for 1 hour.

6. To serve, cut tart into wedges; place on individual serving plates. Poke hole with toothpick in shortest side of each wedge of tart. Insert chocolate stick piece into each hole to resemble stem of tree.

Yield: 16 servings

NUTRITION INFORMATION PER SERVING
Serving Size: ⅟₁₆ of Recipe; Calories 310; Calories from Fat 180 % Daily Value: Total Fat 20g 31%; Saturated Fat 12g 60%; Cholesterol 30mg 10%; Sodium 85mg 4%; Total Carbohydrate 31g 10%; Dietary Fiber 1g 4%; Sugars 25g; Protein 2g; Vitamin A 6%; Vitamin C 0%; Calcium 4%; Iron 6% Dietary Exchanges: 1 Starch, 4 Fat, 1 Other Carbohydrate, 2 Carbohydrate Choices

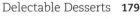

individual lemon-lime cream tarts

Prep Time: 30 minutes   (Ready in 45 minutes)

crust

1 refrigerated pie crust
(from 15-oz. pkg.), softened
as directed on package

filling

1 (3-oz.) pkg. cream cheese,
softened

2 tablespoons powdered sugar

2 tablespoons whipping cream

1 teaspoon grated lime peel

¼ cup lemon curd
(from 10-oz. jar)

garnish

Whipped cream

Strips of lime peel

1. Heat oven to 450°F. Remove pie crust from pouch. Unfold crust; press out fold lines. Cut four 4-inch rounds from crust. Press each round into 4-inch tart pan; prick bottom with fork. Bake at 450°F. for 5 to 9 minutes or until golden brown. Cool 15 minutes or until completely cooled.

2. Meanwhile, in small bowl, combine cream cheese, powdered sugar and whipping cream; beat until smooth. Divide evenly into cooled tart shells.

3. In small bowl, stir grated lime peel into lemon curd until smooth. Spoon evenly over cream cheese mixture in shells to within ¼ inch of edges. Garnish with whipped cream and lime peel strips.

Yield: 4 tarts

NUTRITION INFORMATION PER SERVING
Serving Size: 1 Tart; Calories 395; Calories from Fat 235 **% Daily Value:** Total Fat 26g 40%; Saturated Fat 13g 65%; Cholesterol 60mg 20%; Sodium 320mg 13%; Total Carbohydrate 36g 12%; Dietary Fiber 0g 0%; Sugars 11g; Protein 4g; Vitamin A 10%; Vitamin C 0%; Calcium 2%; Iron 2% **Dietary Exchanges:** 1½ Starch, 5 Fat, 1 Other Carbohydrate, 2½ Carbohydrate Choices

pomegranate tartlets

Prep Time: 45 minutes   (Ready in 1 hour 45 minutes)

crust

3 refrigerated pie crusts
(from two 15-oz. pkg.), softened
as directed on package

topping

1 pomegranate

filling

1 (3-oz.) pkg. vanilla pudding
and pie filling mix (not instant)

1¾ cups whipping cream

2 tablespoons dark rum or
½ to ¾ teaspoon rum extract

1 teaspoon powdered sugar

1. Heat oven to 450°F. Remove pie crusts from pouches. Unfold crusts; press out fold lines. With 2½-inch round cutter, cut crusts into 36 rounds. Press each round into miniature muffin cup. Bake at 450°F. for 7 to 9 minutes or until lightly browned. Remove tartlet shells from pan; place on wire racks. Cool 10 minutes.

2. Meanwhile, cut pomegranate in half; remove and reserve seeds. Set aside.

3. In medium saucepan, combine pudding mix and whipping cream; stir with wire whisk to blend. Cook over medium heat for about 5 minutes or until mixture comes to a boil, stirring constantly. Remove from heat. Stir in rum.

4. Immediately spoon about 2 rounded teaspoons filling into each tartlet shell. Top each with about 1 teaspoon pomegranate seeds. Cover loosely; refrigerate at least 1 hour or until serving time. Just before serving, sprinkle tartlets with powdered sugar.

Yield: 36 tartlets

Family Ties

When it comes to extracting the pomegranate seeds, engage the help of your family. Trim away the crown of the pomegranate and cut into the rind in a few places. Soak the fruit in cold water for five minutes. While it is underwater, break it into sections and separate the seeds—careful, they're slippery! Remove the membrane that floats to the surface, and strain the water to collect the seeds.

NUTRITION INFORMATION PER SERVING
Serving Size: 1 Tartlet; Calories 125; Calories from Fat 70 % **Daily Value:** Total Fat 8g 12%; Saturated Fat 4g 20%; Cholesterol 15mg 5%; Sodium 90mg 4%; Total Carbohydrate 12g 4%; Dietary Fiber 0g 0%; Sugars 3g; Protein 1g; Vitamin A 3%; Vitamin C 0%; Calcium 0%; Iron 0% **Dietary Exchanges:** 1½ Fat, 1 Other Carbohydrate, 1 Carbohydrate Choice

orange crème dessert
with ruby cranberry sauce

Prep Time: 40 minutes   (Ready in 3 hours 40 minutes)

12 chocolate-covered graham crackers, finely crushed (about 1 cup)

2 cups fresh or frozen cranberries

¾ cup sugar

1 teaspoon cornstarch

¾ cup water

1 envelope unflavored gelatin

¼ cup orange juice

4 (6-oz.) containers orange crème low-fat yogurt (2 cups)

2 teaspoons grated orange peel

2 cups frozen light whipped topping, thawed

1. Heat oven to 375°F. Spray 9-inch springform pan with non-stick cooking spray. Press cracker crumbs evenly in bottom of sprayed pan. Bake at 375°F. for 7 minutes. Place in refrigerator or freezer until completely cooled.

2. Meanwhile, in medium saucepan, combine cranberries, sugar, cornstarch and water; mix well. Bring to a boil over medium heat, stirring constantly. Reduce heat to low; simmer 10 to 15 minutes or until cranberries pop, stirring occasionally. Cool 15 minutes. Refrigerate until serving time.

3. In small saucepan, combine gelatin and orange juice; let stand 2 minutes. Place saucepan over low heat; stir until gelatin is dissolved.

4. In blender container, combine yogurt and orange peel; blend until smooth. With blender running, add gelatin mixture. Cover; blend at High speed for 15 to 20 seconds or until combined. Spoon into medium bowl. Gently stir in whipped topping. Spoon and gently spread over cooled crust. Refrigerate 3 hours or until set.

5. To serve, run knife around edge of dessert; remove side of pan. Cut dessert into wedges; place on individual dessert plates. Top each with 2 tablespoons cranberry mixture.

Yield: 12 servings

NUTRITION INFORMATION PER SERVING
Serving Size: ½₁₂ of Recipe; Calories 185; Calories from Fat 35 % **Daily Value:** Total Fat 4g 6%; Saturated Fat 3g 15%; Cholesterol 5mg 2%; Sodium 65mg 3%; Total Carbohydrate 33g 11%; Dietary Fiber 1g 4%; Sugars 28g; Protein 4g; Vitamin A 2%; Vitamin C 4%; Calcium 10%; Iron 0% **Dietary Exchanges:** 1 Starch, 1 Fat, 1 Other Carbohydrate, 2 Carbohydrate Choices

Do-Ahead
This indulgent but light dessert can be prepared a day ahead. Just cover and refrigerate it until you're ready to serve. Don't forget to add the cranberry mixture.

candy cane heart ornaments

1. Hot-glue two wrapped candy canes together to form a heart shape.

2. Attach ribbon bow and tied ribbon to be used as a hanger.

3. Let dry about 15 minutes to set.

eggnog ice cream dessert

Prep Time: 25 minutes   (Ready in 4 hours 55 minutes)

24 gingersnap cookies

½ cup chopped pecans

¼ cup butter, melted

3 pints (6 cups) vanilla ice cream, softened

1½ teaspoons nutmeg

1½ teaspoons rum extract

16 pecan halves, toasted

1. Heat oven to 350°F. In food processor bowl with metal blade, combine cookies and chopped pecans; process until finely ground. Add butter; process until mixed. Press mixture in bottom and 1 inch up sides of ungreased 9-inch spring-form pan.

2. Bake at 350°F. for 8 to 10 minutes or until edges are lightly browned. Cool 30 minutes or until completely cooled.

3. In large bowl, combine softened ice cream, nutmeg and rum extract; stir until blended. Spread evenly in crust-lined pan. Place pecan halves around top edge of dessert. Cover; freeze at least 4 hours or up to 2 weeks.

4. To serve, let dessert stand at room temperature for 15 minutes. Run knife around edge of dessert; remove side of pan. Cut into wedges to serve.

Yield: 16 servings

Special Touch

For authentic flavor, use frozen custard for this dessert. Custard is different from many ice creams because it contains eggs. You could also try making this creamy dessert with French vanilla ice cream, which is tradition-ally made from custard.

raspberry cream heart

Prep Time: 35 minutes   (Ready in 1 hour 5 minutes)

1 (15-oz.) pkg. refrigerated pie crusts, softened as directed on package

1 (8-oz.) pkg. cream cheese, softened

¼ cup powdered sugar

1 (14-oz.) jar strawberry pie glaze

2½ cups fresh raspberries

1 teaspoon powdered sugar

1. Heat oven to 450°F. Remove 1 crust from pouch. Place on ungreased cookie sheet; press out fold lines. Make paper pattern for 11×10-inch heart. With paper pattern as a guide, cut crust into heart shape. Generously prick crust with fork.

2. Bake at 450°F. for 8 to 10 minutes or until light golden brown. Cool 15 minutes. Repeat with remaining crust.

3. In small bowl, combine cream cheese and ¼ cup powdered sugar; beat until smooth. Place 1 cooled crust on serving plate; spread with cream cheese mixture.

4. Reserve ½ cup of the pie glaze. Spread remaining pie glaze over cream cheese mixture. Top with second crust. Spread reserved ½ cup glaze over top crust. Arrange raspberries, stem side down, over top. Sprinkle with 1 teaspoon powdered sugar.

Yield: 8 servings

NUTRITION INFORMATION PER SERVING
Serving Size: ⅛ of Recipe; Calories 585; Calories from Fat 295 **% Daily Value:** Total Fat 33g 51%; Saturated Fat 21g 105%; Cholesterol 40mg 13%; Sodium 300mg 13%; Total Carbohydrate 68g 23%; Dietary Fiber 2g 8%; Sugars 42g; Protein 4g; Vitamin A 8%; Vitamin C 8%; Calcium 2%; Iron 2% **Dietary Exchanges:** 1½ Starch, 6½ Fat, 3 Other Carbohydrates, 4½ Carbohydrate Choices

Substitution

If you have more strawberry lovers than raspberry lovers on your guest list, use 1 to 2 cups of fresh strawberries in place of the raspberries. Cut the strawberries in half and arrange them, cut side down, over the glaze.

chocolate-cherry cheesecake

Prep Time: 35 minutes (Ready in 5 hours 50 minutes)

crust

2 cups chocolate cookie crumbs

3 tablespoons butter, melted

filling

4 (8-oz.) pkg. cream cheese, softened

3 eggs

¾ cup sugar

½ teaspoon almond extract

½ cup whipping cream

1 (21-oz.) can cherry pie filling

glaze

½ cup whipping cream

1 (6-oz.) pkg. (1 cup) semisweet chocolate chips

1. Heat oven to 325°F. In medium bowl, combine crust ingredients; mix well. Press in bottom and 1 inch up sides of ungreased 10-inch springform pan.

2. Beat cream cheese in large bowl until smooth. Add eggs one at a time, beating well after each addition. Add sugar and almond extract; beat until smooth. Add ½ cup whipping cream; blend well.

3. Spoon 3½ cups cream cheese mixture into crust-lined pan; spread evenly. Carefully spoon 1 cup of the pie filling evenly over cream cheese layer. (Reserve remaining pie filling for topping.) Spoon remaining cream cheese mixture evenly over pie filling.

4. Bake at 325°F. for 1 hour 5 minutes to 1 hour 15 minutes or until center is set. Cool in pan on wire rack for 1 hour.

5. Bring ½ cup whipping cream to a boil in small saucepan. Remove from heat. Stir in chocolate chips until melted.

6. Line cookie sheet with waxed paper. Remove sides of springform pan. Place cooled cheesecake on paper-lined cookie sheet. Spread glaze over cheesecake, allowing some to run down sides. Refrigerate at least 3 hours or overnight. Top individual servings of cheesecake with reserved pie filling.

Yield: 16 servings

NUTRITION INFORMATION PER SERVING
Serving Size: 1/16 of Recipe; Calories 475; Calories from Fat 295 **% Daily Value:** Total Fat 33g 51%; Saturated Fat 20g 100%; Cholesterol 125mg 42%; Sodium 280mg 12%; Total Carbohydrate 37g 12%; Dietary Fiber 1g 4%; Sugars 29g; Protein 8g; Vitamin A 22%; Vitamin C 0%; Calcium 6%; Iron 10% **Dietary Exchanges:** 2½ Starch, 6½ Fat, 2½ Carbohydrate Choices

Substitution

Look for premade cookie crusts in the baking aisle of your grocery store. They don't have quite the same taste, but they're heaven-sent when you're short on time.

chocolate-covered cherry cookies

Prep Time: 1 hour 5 minutes

cookies

½ cup granulated sugar

¾ cup butter, softened

1 teaspoon vanilla

1 egg yolk

1½ cups all-purpose flour

¼ cup unsweetened cocoa

filling

¼ cup butter, softened

1 tablespoon brandy or
½ teaspoon brandy extract

1 cup powdered sugar

topping

36 maraschino cherries with
stems, drained on paper towels

½ cup semisweet chocolate
chips

1 teaspoon vegetable oil

1. Heat oven to 375°F. In large bowl, combine granulated sugar, ¾ cup butter, the vanilla and egg yolk; beat until light and fluffy. Add flour and cocoa; beat until well mixed.

2. Shape rounded teaspoonfuls of dough into 1-inch balls; place 1 inch apart on ungreased cookie sheets. With index finger, make indentation in center of each cookie.

3. Bake at 375°F. for 7 to 9 minutes or until set. Immediately remove from cookie sheets. Cool 10 minutes or until completely cooled.

4. Meanwhile, in medium bowl, combine all filling ingredients; beat until smooth.

5. Spoon about ½ teaspoon filling into center of each cooled cookie. Press cherry into filling.

6. In small saucepan, melt chocolate chips with oil over low heat, stirring constantly. Spoon or drizzle melted chocolate over cherry on each cookie. Let stand until chocolate is set.

Yield: 3 dozen cookies

NUTRITION INFORMATION PER SERVING
Serving Size: 1 Cookie; Calories 110; Calories from Fat 55 **% Daily Value:** Total Fat 6g 9%; Saturated Fat 4g 20%; Cholesterol 20mg 7%; Sodium 35mg 1%; Total Carbohydrate 13g 4%; Dietary Fiber 0g 0%; Sugars 9g; Protein 1g; Vitamin A 4%; Vitamin C 0%; Calcium 0%; Iron 2% **Dietary Exchanges:** 1 Fat, 1 Other Carbohydrate, 1 Carbohydrate Choice

Special Touch

For contrast, try spooning or drizzling melted white chocolate or almond bark over the cherry on each cookie.

cardamom sandwich cookies

Prep Time: 50 minutes (Ready in 1 hour 50 minutes)

cookies

1 cup firmly packed brown sugar

1 cup butter, softened

1 egg

2 cups all-purpose flour

1 teaspoon cardamom

1 teaspoon cinnamon

¼ cup sugar

filling

2 tablespoons butter

1¼ cups powdered sugar

½ teaspoon vanilla

4 to 5 teaspoons milk

1. In large bowl, combine brown sugar and 1 cup butter; beat until light and fluffy. Add egg; blend well. Add flour, cardamom and cinnamon; mix well. If necessary, cover with plastic wrap; refrigerate 1 hour for easier handling.

2. Heat oven to 350°F. Shape dough into 1-inch balls; roll in sugar. Place 2 inches apart on ungreased cookie sheets. For each cookie, dip bottom of glass with textured base in sugar; flatten dough ball to form 1½-inch round.

3. Bake at 350°F. for 6 to 10 minutes or until firm to the touch. Immediately remove from cookie sheets. Cool 15 minutes or until completely cooled.

4. Melt 2 tablespoons butter in medium saucepan over medium heat; cook until light golden brown, stirring constantly. Remove from heat. Stir in all remaining filling ingredients, adding enough milk for desired spreading consistency. For each sandwich cookie, spread about 1 teaspoon filling between 2 cooled cookies.

Yield: 2 dozen sandwich cookies

NUTRITION INFORMATION PER SERVING
Serving Size: 1 Sandwich Cookie;
Calories 185; Calories from Fat 80 % **Daily Value:**
Total Fat 9g 14%; Saturated Fat 5g 25%;
Cholesterol 30mg 10%; Sodium 65mg 3%; Total
Carbohydrate 25g 8%; Dietary Fiber 0g 0%;
Sugars 17g; Protein 1g; Vitamin A 6%;
Vitamin C 0%; Calcium 2%; Iron 4% **Dietary
Exchanges:** 2 Fat, 1½ Other Carbohydrates,
1½ Carbohydrate Choices

Do-Ahead
Filled sandwich cookies may be frozen for up to two months; layer them between sheets of waxed paper in an airtight container. If you hold off on filling the cookies, they may be frozen for up to four months when sealed in an airtight container.

orange spritz

Prep Time: 45 minutes

1 cup butter or margarine, softened

1 cup powdered sugar

½ teaspoon vanilla

1 egg

2⅓ cups all-purpose flour

1 tablespoon grated orange peel

¼ teaspoon salt

1. Heat oven to 400°F. In large bowl, combine butter, powdered sugar, vanilla and egg; beat until light and fluffy. Add flour, orange peel and salt; mix well.

2. Place desired template in cookie press. Fill cookie press with dough. Press dough onto ungreased cookie sheets.

3. Bake at 400°F. for 4 to 7 minutes or until bottoms are light golden brown. Immediately remove from cookie sheets.

Yield: 5 dozen cookies

NUTRITION INFORMATION PER SERVING
Serving Size: 1 Cookie; Calories 55; Calories from Fat 25 % **Daily Value:** Total Fat 3g 5%; Saturated Fat 2g 10%; Cholesterol 10mg 3%; Sodium 30mg 1%; Total Carbohydrate 6g 2%; Dietary Fiber 0g 0%; Sugars 2g; Protein 1g; Vitamin A 2%; Vitamin C 0%; Calcium 0%; Iron 2% **Dietary Exchanges:** ½ Fat, ½ Other Carbohydrate, ½ Carbohydrate Choice

Substitution

To make Chocolate Spritz Cookies, leave out the grated orange peel and use 2 ounces of melted unsweetened chocolate instead.

chocolate-toffee bars

Prep Time: 20 minutes   (Ready in 1 hour 35 minutes)

crust

1 cup all-purpose flour

½ cup firmly packed brown sugar

½ cup butter, softened

topping

1 cup firmly packed brown sugar

2 tablespoons all-purpose flour

1 teaspoon baking powder

2 eggs

1 (6-oz.) pkg. (1 cup) semisweet chocolate chips

½ cup chopped nuts

1. Heat oven to 350°F. Line 13×9-inch pan with heavy-duty foil so foil extends over sides of pan. In small bowl, combine all crust ingredients; blend well. Press in bottom of foil-lined pan. Bake at 350°F. for 8 to 10 minutes or until lightly browned. Cool 5 minutes or until slightly cooled. Increase oven temperature to 375°F.

2. Meanwhile, in medium bowl, combine 1 cup brown sugar, 2 tablespoons flour, the baking powder and eggs; blend well. Stir in chocolate chips and nuts. Pour topping evenly over crust, spreading slightly if necessary.

3. Bake at 375°F. for 13 to 18 minutes or until deep golden brown and center is set. Cool 1 hour or until completely cooled. Cut into bars.

Yield: 36 bars

NUTRITION INFORMATION PER SERVING
Serving Size: 1 Bar; Calories 110; Calories from Fat 45 **% Daily Value:** Total Fat 5g 8%; Saturated Fat 3g 15%; Cholesterol 20mg 7%; Sodium 40mg 2%; Total Carbohydrate 15g 5%; Dietary Fiber 0g 0%; Sugars 12g; Protein 1g; Vitamin A 2%; Vitamin C 0%; Calcium 2%; Iron 2% **Dietary Exchanges:** 1 Fat, 1 Other Carbohydrate, 1 Carbohydrate Choice

Family Ties

If your kids aren't crazy about nuts, feel free to leave them out. You can always toss in an extra ½ cup of chocolate chips to make up the difference.

white chocolate-raspberry bars

Prep Time: 20 minutes   (Ready in 2 hours)

1 (18-oz.) roll refrigerated sugar cookie dough

1¼ cups white chocolate chunks or white vanilla chips

1 (12-oz.) jar (¾ cup) raspberry jam or preserves

1 teaspoon vegetable oil

1. Heat oven to 350°F. Break up cookie dough into ungreased 13×9-inch pan. With floured fingers, press dough evenly in bottom of pan to form crust. Sprinkle 1 cup of the white chocolate chunks over crust; press firmly into dough.

2. Bake at 350°F. for 16 to 20 minutes or until light golden brown.

3. Remove partially baked crust from oven. Spread jam evenly over crust. Return to oven; bake an additional 10 minutes. Cool 1 hour or until completely cooled.

4. In small resealable plastic bag, combine remaining ¼ cup white chocolate chunks and the oil; partially seal bag. Microwave on High for 30 seconds. Squeeze bag until chunks are smooth. If necessary, microwave an additional 15 to 30 seconds.

5. Cut small hole in bottom corner of bag. Squeeze bag gently to drizzle white chocolate over bars. Refrigerate about 20 minutes or until chocolate is set. Cut into bars. Serve at room temperature.

Yield: 48 bars

NUTRITION INFORMATION PER SERVING
Serving Size: 1 Bar; Calories 105; Calories from Fat 35 **% Daily Value:** Total Fat 4g 6%; Saturated Fat 2g 10%; Cholesterol 0mg 0%; Sodium 45mg 2%; Total Carbohydrate 16g 5%; Dietary Fiber 0g 0%; Sugars 12g; Protein 1g; Vitamin A 0%; Vitamin C 0%; Calcium 2%; Iron 2% **Dietary Exchanges:** 1 Fat, 1 Other Carbohydrate, 1 Carbohydrate Choice

Family Ties
Get the kids involved in making this easy, fun recipe. What's not to like about getting your hands full of flour and smooshing cookie dough in a pan? Older children can drizzle the white chocolate over the top.

mint-kissed meringues

Prep Time: 25 minutes   (Ready in 2 hours 25 minutes)

2 egg whites

¼ teaspoon cream of tartar

⅛ teaspoon salt

½ cup sugar

¼ teaspoon mint extract

3 to 5 drops green food color

Multicolored candy sprinkles, if desired

1. Heat oven to 200°F. Grease 2 large cookie sheets. In small bowl, combine egg whites, cream of tartar and salt; beat with electric mixer at medium speed until foamy.

2. Increase mixer speed to high; add sugar 1 tablespoon at a time, beating until meringue is very stiff and glossy, and sugar is dissolved. Beat in mint extract. Fold in food color 1 drop at a time until of desired color.

3. Use disposable decorating bag or gallon-sized food storage plastic bag with ½-inch hole cut in bottom corner of bag. If desired, fit large star tip in corner. Spoon meringue into bag; twist top of bag to seal. Squeeze bag to pipe meringue into 1-inch puffs on greased cookie sheets. Sprinkle each with candy sprinkles.

4. Place cookie sheets on center rack in oven. Bake at 200°F. for 2 hours. Immediately remove cookies from cookie sheets; place on wire racks. Cool 5 minutes or until completely cooled.

Yield: 4 dozen cookies

NUTRITION INFORMATION PER SERVING
Serving Size: 1 Cookie; Calories 10; Calories from Fat 0 **% Daily Value:** Total Fat 0g 0%; Saturated Fat 0g 0%; Cholesterol 0mg 0%; Sodium 10mg 0%; Total Carbohydrate 2g 1%; Dietary Fiber 0g 0%; Sugars 2g; Protein 0g; Vitamin A 0%; Vitamin C 0%; Calcium 0%; Iron 0% **Dietary Exchanges:** Free, 0 Carbohydrate Choice

Do-Ahead

These minty meringues can be made up to one month ahead and frozen. For maximum freshness, store them in an airtight container.

chocolate-covered cheesecake bites

Prep Time: 1 hour 20 minutes   (Ready in 5 hours 55 minutes)

crust

1 cup graham cracker crumbs

¼ cup chopped pecans

¼ cup butter, melted

filling

2 (8-oz.) pkg. cream cheese, softened

½ cup sugar

1 teaspoon grated orange peel

¼ cup sour cream

½ teaspoon vanilla

2 eggs

coating

24 oz. semisweet chocolate, chopped

3 tablespoons shortening

1. Heat oven to 300°F. Line 8-inch square pan with heavy-duty foil so foil extends over sides of pan; spray foil with nonstick cooking spray. In small bowl, combine all crust ingredients; mix well. Press in bottom of sprayed foil-lined pan.

2. Beat cream cheese in large bowl until smooth. Add all remaining filling ingredients; beat until well combined. Pour filling over crust.

3. Bake at 300°F. for 40 to 45 minutes or until edges are set. Center will be soft but will set when cool. Refrigerate 1½ hours or until chilled. Freeze cheesecake about 2 hours or until firm.

4. Remove cheesecake from pan by lifting foil. Cut into 48 pieces; remove from foil and place on sheet of waxed paper.

5. In small saucepan, melt coating ingredients over low heat, stirring frequently until smooth. Cool 2 to 3 minutes or until slightly cooled. Place in 2-cup measuring cup.

6. Spear each cheesecake bite with fork; dip in melted chocolate to cover bottom and sides, letting excess drip off. Place on waxed paper.

7. Spoon about 1 teaspoon melted chocolate over each bite, smoothing top with back of spoon. Let stand about 20 minutes or until firm. Store in refrigerator.

Yield: 48 bites

Substitution

Other kinds of crumbs can be used to make the crust for these bite-sized treats. Try chocolate or cinnamon graham crackers, or chocolate or vanilla wafers.

sparkling settings

1. Spray-paint large pinecones gold or silver.

2. Tie a bright ribbon around the pinecone.

3. Write guest's name on a small piece of paper
   and nestle it in pinecone.

caramel candy bars

Prep Time: 35 minutes   (Ready in 2 hours)

1½ cups firmly packed brown sugar

1½ cups butter, softened

1 cup quick-cooking rolled oats

1 cup crisp rice cereal

2 cups all-purpose flour

1 teaspoon baking soda

½ teaspoon salt

35 vanilla caramels, unwrapped

⅓ cup milk

1 (14-oz.) pkg. red and green candy-coated milk chocolate pieces

1. Heat oven to 350°F. Spray 13×9-inch pan with nonstick cooking spray. In large bowl, combine brown sugar and butter; beat until smooth. Stir in oats and cereal. Add flour, baking soda and salt; mix until well blended. Reserve 3 cups oat mixture for topping. Press remaining mixture in bottom of sprayed pan. Bake at 350°F. for 10 minutes.

2. Meanwhile, in small saucepan, combine caramels and milk; heat over low heat until caramels are melted and mixture is smooth, stirring constantly.

3. Remove pan from oven. Sprinkle 1 cup of the chocolate pieces evenly over base. Drizzle with caramel mixture, being careful not to let caramel touch sides of pan. Drop reserved oat mixture by heaping teaspoonfuls over caramel mixture. Sprinkle with remaining chocolate pieces.

4. Return to oven; bake an additional 20 to 24 minutes or until center is set and top is golden brown. Cool 1 hour or until completely cooled. Cut into bars.

Yield: 32 bars

Special Touch

Chocolate lovers may want to drizzle these crunchy bars with cooled melted chocolate. You could also use candy-coated peanut butter pieces instead of the candy-coated milk chocolate pieces.

Caramel Candy Bars

layered mint-chocolate fudge

Prep Time: 50 minutes   (Ready in 2 hours 50 minutes)

4½ cups sugar

½ cup butter

1 (12-oz.) can evaporated milk

4½ cups miniature marshmallows

18 oz. (3 cups) semisweet chocolate chips

2 oz. unsweetened chocolate, cut into pieces

1 teaspoon vanilla

1 (6-oz.) pkg. white chocolate baking bar, cut into pieces

⅛ teaspoon peppermint extract

⅛ teaspoon green paste icing color

2 tablespoons chocolate sprinkles

1. Line 15×10×1-inch baking pan with foil so foil extends over sides of pan; grease foil. In large saucepan, combine sugar, butter and evaporated milk; cook and stir over medium heat until sugar is dissolved. Bring to a full boil, stirring constantly. Without stirring, boil 5 minutes over medium heat.

2. Remove from heat. Add marshmallows, stirring constantly until mixture is smooth. Remove 2 cups mixture; place in medium saucepan. Set aside.

3. To mixture in large saucepan, add chocolate chips, unsweetened chocolate and vanilla; stir until chocolate is melted and mixture is smooth. Quickly spread mixture in greased foil-lined pan.

4. To reserved mixture in medium saucepan, add white chocolate, peppermint extract and green icing color; stir until chocolate is melted and mixture is smooth. Pour evenly over fudge in pan; spread gently to cover. Sprinkle with chocolate sprinkles. Refrigerate 2 hours or until firm.

5. Remove fudge from pan by lifting foil; remove foil. Cut into squares.

Yield: 72 candies

NUTRITION INFORMATION PER SERVING
Serving Size: 1 Candy; Calories 135; Calories from Fat 45 **% Daily Value:** Total Fat 5g 8%; Saturated Fat 3g 15%; Cholesterol 5mg 2%; Sodium 20mg 1%; Total Carbohydrate 22g 7%; Dietary Fiber 0g 0%; Sugars 20g; Protein 1g; Vitamin A 0%; Vitamin C 0%; Calcium 2%; Iron 2% **Dietary Exchanges:** 1 Fat, 1½ Other Carbohydrates, 1½ Carbohydrate Choices

Special Touch
This rich fudge makes a great gift. For old-fashioned flair, wrap individual pieces of fudge in small squares of parchment paper, waxed paper or aluminum foil.

spiced walnut brittle

Prep Time: 15 minutes   (Ready in 45 minutes)

1 cup sugar

½ cup light corn syrup

1 cup coarsely chopped walnuts

½ teaspoon cinnamon

1 teaspoon butter

1 teaspoon vanilla

1 teaspoon baking soda

1. Butter cookie sheet. In 8-cup microwave-safe measuring cup or medium microwave-safe bowl, combine sugar and corn syrup; mix well. Microwave on High for 4 minutes. Stir; microwave on High for an additional 3 to 5 minutes or until mixture turns light brown.

2. Add walnuts, cinnamon, butter and vanilla; blend well. Microwave on High for 1 minute.

3. Add baking soda; stir until light and foamy. Pour onto buttered cookie sheet. Cool 30 minutes or until firm. Break brittle into 2-inch pieces. Store in tightly covered container.

Yield: 20 pieces

Special Touch

To make the walnuts even more flavorful, toast them before adding them to the mix. To toast, spread the nuts in a single layer in a shallow pan and bake at 350°F. for about 7 minutes, shaking the pan once or twice, until the nuts are fragrant and golden. Let them cool completely before using.

NUTRITION INFORMATION PER SERVING
Serving Size: 1 Piece; Calories 110; Calories from Fat 35 **% Daily Value:** Total Fat 4g 6%; Saturated Fat 0g 0%; Cholesterol 0mg 0%; Sodium 75mg 3%; Total Carbohydrate 17g 6%; Dietary Fiber 0g 0%; Sugars 13g; Protein 1g; Vitamin A 0%; Vitamin C 0%; Calcium 0%; Iron 0% **Dietary Exchanges:** 1 Fat, 1 Other Carbohydrate, 1 Carbohydrate Choice

cranberry-walnut white fudge

Prep Time: 20 minutes   (Ready in 1 hour 20 minutes)

1 (12-oz.) pkg. (2 cups) white vanilla chips

½ cup powdered sugar

½ cup vanilla ready-to-spread frosting (from 16-oz. can)

1 (3-oz.) pkg. cream cheese, softened

¾ cup chopped walnuts

⅓ cup sweetened dried cranberries

1 teaspoon grated orange peel

1. Line 9-inch square pan with foil so foil extends over sides of pan; spray foil lightly with nonstick cooking spray. Melt vanilla chips in small saucepan over low heat, stirring until smooth. Remove from heat.

2. In medium bowl, combine powdered sugar, frosting and cream cheese; blend well. Stir in melted chips, walnuts, cranberries and orange peel. Spread in sprayed foil-lined pan. Refrigerate about 1 hour or until firm.

3. Remove fudge from pan by lifting foil; remove foil. Cut into squares. Serve fudge at room temperature.

Yield: 36 candies

NUTRITION INFORMATION PER SERVING
Serving Size: 1 Candy; Calories 110; Calories from Fat 55 **% Daily Value:** Total Fat 6g 9%; Saturated Fat 3g 15%; Cholesterol 5mg 2%; Sodium 15mg 1%; Total Carbohydrate 13g 4%; Dietary Fiber 0g 0%; Sugars 12g; Protein 1g; Vitamin A 0%; Vitamin C 0%; Calcium 2%; Iron 0% **Dietary Exchanges:** 1 Fat, 1 Other Carbohydrate, 1 Carbohydrate Choice

Do-Ahead

The fudge can be frozen for up to three months. Let it cool after baking, then layer small squares between sheets of waxed paper in an airtight container.

peppermint-bark hearts

Prep Time: 20 minutes   (Ready in 50 minutes)

18 (2½-inch) peppermint candy canes, unwrapped

5 oz. vanilla-flavored candy coating or almond bark, chopped

2 teaspoons crushed peppermint candy canes

1. Line cookie sheet with waxed paper. Arrange candy canes on waxed paper in groups of 2 with ends touching to form heart shapes.

2. Place candy coating in 2-cup microwave-safe measuring cup. Microwave on Medium for 2 to 3 minutes, stirring once halfway through cooking time. Stir until melted and smooth.

3. Spoon or pipe candy coating into centers of hearts to fill spaces. Sprinkle with crushed candy canes. Cool 30 minutes or until set.

Yield: 9 candy hearts

NUTRITION INFORMATION PER SERVING
Serving Size: 1 Candy Heart; Calories 110; Calories from Fat 45 **% Daily Value:** Total Fat 5g 8%; Saturated Fat 3g 15%; Cholesterol 5mg 2%; Sodium 15mg 1%; Total Carbohydrate 15g 5%; Dietary Fiber 0g 0%; Sugars 16g; Protein 1g; Vitamin A 0%; Vitamin C 0%; Calcium 2%; Iron 0% **Dietary Exchanges:** 1 Fat, 1 Other Carbohydrate, 1 Carbohydrate Choice

Substitution

Chocolate-flavored candy coating can be used instead of vanilla-flavored candy coating. Or make two batches— one of each!

almost-instant buckeyes

Prep Time: 30 minutes   (Ready in 1 hour 20 minutes)

1 (10-oz.) pkg. peanut butter chips

1 (16-oz.) can vanilla ready-to-spread frosting

1 (12-oz.) pkg. light cocoa candy melts or coating wafers

1. Line cookie sheets with waxed paper. Melt peanut butter chips in medium saucepan over low heat, stirring constantly. Remove from heat. Stir in frosting. Let stand about 10 minutes or until cool enough to handle.

2. Roll mixture into 1-inch balls; place on waxed-paper-lined cookie sheet. Refrigerate 15 minutes.

3. Meanwhile, melt cocoa candy melts as directed on package.

4. Pierce each ball with wooden skewer or toothpick; dip in melted candy, leaving small area around skewer uncoated. Place dipped ball on waxed-paper-lined cookie sheet, pushing candy off skewer with tines of fork. (If desired, smooth skewer mark with finger.) If melted candy sets up while dipping, reheat in microwave on Low power. Let stand 5 minutes or until set.

Yield: 6 dozen candies

NUTRITION INFORMATION PER SERVING
Serving Size: 1 Candy; Calories 80; Calories from Fat 35 **% Daily Value:** Total Fat 4g 6%; Saturated Fat 2g 10%; Cholesterol 0mg 0%; Sodium 10mg 0%; Total Carbohydrate 10g 3%; Dietary Fiber 0g 0%; Sugars 9g; Protein 1g; Vitamin A 0%; Vitamin C 0%; Calcium 0%; Iron 0% **Dietary Exchanges:** 1 Fat, ½ Other Carbohydrate, ½ Carbohydrate Choice

Special Touch
These peanut-buttery balls make great Christmas or hostess gifts. Arrange in a box or a holiday tin lined with parchment or waxed paper.

christmas tree candy pops

Prep Time: 35 minutes

1 cup (6½ oz.) green candy melts or coating wafers

Small candies and/or decorating icing

Flat wooden sticks with rounded ends

Plastic wrap

1. Line cookie sheets with foil. Melt candy melts as directed on package. Spoon melted candy into resealable food storage plastic bag or small plastic squeeze bottle; seal bag or cover bottle. If using bags, cut small hole in one bottom corner.

2. On foil-lined cookie sheets, squeeze out melted candy to create 3-inch tree shapes about ¼ inch thick. Immediately decorate as desired with candies or icing.

3. Freeze 1 minute to set. When set, peel candy pops from foil. To attach shapes to wooden sticks, place small amount of melted coating on stick; gently press shape onto stick. Let stand 5 minutes or until set. Wrap each in plastic wrap.

Yield: 24 candy pops

NUTRITION INFORMATION PER SERVING
Serving Size: 1 Candy Pop; Calories 75; Calories from Fat 35 **% Daily Value:** Total Fat 4g 6%; Saturated Fat 3g 15%; Cholesterol 5mg 2%; Sodium 10mg 0%; Total Carbohydrate 9g 3%; Dietary Fiber 0g 0%; Sugars 9g; Protein 1g; Vitamin A 0%; Vitamin C 0%; Calcium 2%; Iron 0% **Dietary Exchanges:** 1 Fat, ½ Other Carbohydrate, ½ Carbohydrate Choice

Special Touch

Instead of stashing these cute candy pops out of sight, why not show them off by propping them up in round coconut and marshmallow-covered cream-filled chocolate cakes?

8 *Homemade Gifts from the Kitchen*

Marzipan-Stuffed Apricots
in Chocolate 228

Crispy Chocolate Treats in a Jar 229

White Fudge Cookie Cutter Gifts 231

Merry Ginger Muffin Mix 232

Orange-Spice Coffee Mix 234

Spiced Pear Chutney 235

Salsa and Black Bean Dip 236

Honey-Sage Whipped Butter 237

Hot Buttered Rum Sauce 239

Cranberry Mustard 240

Caramel Pecan Sauce 241

Holiday Spiced Nuts 242

marzipan-stuffed apricots in chocolate

Prep Time: 40 minutes

4 oz. marzipan

24 large dried whole Mediterranean apricots

⅓ cup (4 oz.) dark cocoa candy melts or coating wafers

1. Roll marzipan into 24 small balls. Stuff 1 ball of marzipan into opening in each apricot where pit was removed. Press apricot closed, flattening slightly.

2. Melt candy melts as directed on package. Dip each apricot halfway in melted candy; place on sheet of waxed paper. Let stand about 5 minutes or until candy coating is set.

Yield: 24 candies

Substitution

This recipe calls for Mediterranean apricots because they are treated with sulphur so their color stays vibrantly orange. Any dried apricots will do; just make sure they're whole or you won't be able to stuff them.

NUTRITION INFORMATION PER SERVING
Serving Size: 1 Candy; Calories 70; Calories from Fat 25 **% Daily Value:** Total Fat 3g 5%; Saturated Fat 1g 5%; Cholesterol 0mg 0%; Sodium 0mg 0%; Total Carbohydrate 10g 3%; Dietary Fiber 1g 4%; Sugars 7g; Protein 1g; Vitamin A 10%; Vitamin C 0%; Calcium 0%; Iron 4% **Dietary Exchanges:** ½ Starch, ½ Fat, ½ Carbohydrate Choice

crispy chocolate treats in a jar

Prep Time: 10 minutes

⅔ cup miniature candy-coated semisweet chocolate baking bits

1 (1-quart) glass jar with cover

1 cup Wheat Chex® Cereal

½ cup raisins

½ cup peanuts

⅓ cup butterscotch chips

1. Place ⅓ cup of the baking bits in resealable food storage plastic bag or wrap in sheet of plastic wrap. Place in bottom of jar, hiding zipper section underneath bag.

2. Layer with ½ cup of the cereal squares, the raisins, peanuts, remaining ½ cup cereal squares, remaining ⅓ cup baking bits and the butterscotch chips. Press down gently while layering to make sure all ingredients fit. Cover; decorate as desired. Write directions (below) on decorative card; attach to container.

Crispy Chocolate Treats

Line cookie sheets with waxed paper. Place ¼ cup creamy peanut butter in medium saucepan. Spoon in butterscotch chips and top layer of baking bits. Cook over low heat, stirring constantly until melted. Remove from heat. Stir in remaining contents of jar except for baking bits in plastic bag. Drop mixture by rounded tablespoonfuls onto waxed-paper-lined cookie sheets. Sprinkle remaining baking bits in bag evenly over top of cookies. Refrigerate about 10 minutes or until set.

Yield: 20 cookies

NUTRITION INFORMATION PER SERVING
Serving Size: 1 Cookie; Calories 70; Calories from Fat 35 **% Daily Value:** Total Fat 4g 6%; Saturated Fat 1g 5%; Cholesterol 0mg 0%; Sodium 60mg 3%; Total Carbohydrate 7g 2%; Dietary Fiber 1g 4%; Sugars 3g; Protein 2g; Vitamin A 0%; Vitamin C 0%; Calcium 0%; Iron 6% **Dietary Exchanges:** ½ Starch, ½ Fat, ½ Carbohydrate Choice

Family Ties
Tie the recipe and a big bow onto the jar and give it to your favorite child, or arrange for a child to give the jar to someone special. Making the cookies with children is part of the fun of the gift.

white fudge cookie cutter gifts

Prep Time: 25 minutes   (Ready in 1 hour 25 minutes)

5 open metal 6-inch cookie cutters

1 (12-oz.) pkg. (2 cups) white vanilla chips

1 (16-oz.) can vanilla ready-to-spread frosting

½ teaspoon cherry extract

Decorating icing

Colored sugar

Candies

Cellophane or plastic wrap

Ribbon

1. Line large cookie sheet with foil; spray foil with nonstick cooking spray. Generously spray open metal 6-inch cookie cutters; place on sprayed foil-lined cookie sheet.

2. Melt white vanilla chips in medium saucepan over low heat, stirring frequently until smooth. Remove from heat. Stir in frosting and cherry extract.

3. Fill each cookie cutter with ½ cup melted mixture. Refrigerate about 1 hour or until firm. Decorate as desired using icing, colored sugar and candies.

4. Wrap each fudge-filled cookie cutter gift with cellophane; tie with ribbon. Store in refrigerator.

Yield: 5 gifts; 4 servings each

NUTRITION INFORMATION PER SERVING
Serving Size: ¹⁄₂₀ of Recipe; Calories 200; Calories from Fat 80 % **Daily Value:** Total Fat 9g 14%; Saturated Fat 6g 30%; Cholesterol 5mg 2%; Sodium 25mg 1%; Total Carbohydrate 29g 10%; Dietary Fiber 0g 0%; Sugars 29g; Protein 1g; Vitamin A 0%; Vitamin C 0%; Calcium 4%; Iron 0%, 2 Other Carbohydrates, 2 Carbohydrate Choices

Special Touch
Look for lightweight, narrow cellophane bags printed with seasonal designs at kitchen supply stores during the holidays. The bags make wrapping these cookie cutter gifts a breeze.

merry ginger muffin mix

Prep Time: 10 minutes

6 cups all-purpose flour

2 cups sugar

¾ cup instant nonfat dry milk

⅓ cup finely chopped crystallized ginger

3 teaspoons baking powder

2 teaspoons salt

1 teaspoon ground ginger

¾ teaspoon baking soda

1. In large bowl, combine all ingredients; mix well. Store in tightly covered container or resealable food storage plastic bag at room temperature or in a cool, dry place.

2. For gift giving, measure 2 cups of mix by dipping cup into mix and leveling off; place in tightly covered container or resealable food storage plastic bag. Write directions (below) on decorative card; attach to container.

Merry Ginger Muffins

Heat oven to 400°F. Line 12 medium muffin cups with paper baking cups. Combine muffin mix from container, ⅔ cup water, ⅓ cup oil and 1 slightly beaten egg in medium bowl; stir just until dry ingredients are moistened. Do not overmix. Divide evenly into paper-lined muffin cups. Bake 15 to 17 minutes or until toothpick inserted in center comes out clean. Immediately remove from pan. Serve warm.

Yield: 4 dozen muffins

Special Touch

There are lots of creative ways to "wrap" this muffin mix and give it as a gift. Use a jelly jar tied with a colorful ribbon, or place the mix (in a resealable food storage plastic bag, of course) in a red or green paper bag designed with your own label. Include the mix with a muffin tin and holiday baking cups in a basket. When all is said and done, don't forget to provide the recipe!

NUTRITION INFORMATION PER SERVING
Serving Size: 1 Muffin; Calories 165; Calories from Fat 65 **% Daily Value:** Total Fat 7g 11%; Saturated Fat 1g 5%; Cholesterol 20mg 7%; Sodium 115mg 5%; Total Carbohydrate 22g 7%; Dietary Fiber 0g 0%; Sugars 10g; Protein 3g; Vitamin A 0%; Vitamin C 0%; Calcium 4%; Iron 4% **Dietary Exchanges:** 1 Starch, 1 Fat, ½ Other Carbohydrate, 1½ Carbohydrate Choices

A Gift For You

Merry Ginger
Muffin Mix

Recipes

orange-spice coffee mix

Prep Time: 5 minutes

½ cup instant espresso coffee granules, or instant coffee granules or crystals

¼ cup sugar

¼ cup nondairy creamer

3 teaspoons dried orange peel

3 teaspoons cinnamon

1 teaspoon nutmeg

In small bowl, combine all ingredients; mix well. Store in tightly covered container or resealable food storage plastic bag. Write directions (below) on decorative card; attach to container.

Orange-Spice Coffee

Spoon 1 to 2 tablespoons mix into cup. Add ¾ cup boiling water; stir until dissolved. If desired, garnish with whipped cream and dash of nutmeg or cinnamon. Serve immediately.

Yield: 1 cup mix; 8 to 16 (¾-cup) servings

NUTRITION INFORMATION PER SERVING
Serving Size: ¾ Cup Hot Beverage; Calories 20; Calories from Fat 0 **% Daily Value:** Total Fat 0g 0%; Saturated Fat 0g 0%; Cholesterol 0mg 0%; Sodium 0mg 0%; Total Carbohydrate 5g 2%; Dietary Fiber 0g 0%; Sugars 3g; Protein 0g; Vitamin A 0%; Vitamin C 0%; Calcium 0%; Iron 0% **Dietary Exchanges:** Free, 0 Carbohydrate Choice

Special Touch

This mix makes a thoughtful gift for coffee lovers on your holiday list. Put the mix in a resealable food storage plastic bag, and nestle the bag in a pretty coffee cup or mug along with a gift certificate for the recipient's favorite java joint.

spiced pear chutney

Prep Time: 25 minutes   (Ready in 4 hours 10 minutes)

¾ cup firmly packed brown sugar

¾ cup cider vinegar

3 firm large pears (1½ lb.), chopped

½ cup chopped onion (1 medium)

½ cup chopped red bell pepper

¼ cup golden or dark raisins

1 tablespoon grated gingerroot

½ teaspoon cinnamon

½ teaspoon coriander

1. In large saucepan, combine brown sugar and vinegar; mix well. Bring to a boil. Reduce heat; simmer 10 minutes.

2. Stir in all remaining ingredients. Return to a boil. Reduce heat; simmer 45 minutes or until thickened, stirring occasionally. Cool slightly. Refrigerate at least 3 hours or until chilled. Store in a covered container in refrigerator for up to 2 weeks.

Yield: 4 cups

Special Touch
When giving food gifts, it's always nice to attach a label. Write your name, list the ingredients and make some suggestions for using the gift (this chutney nicely complements baked ham, pork chops and roast turkey). On this recipe's label, be sure to note that the chutney should be refrigerated.

NUTRITION INFORMATION PER SERVING
Serving Size: 2 Tablespoons; Calories 20; Calories from Fat 0 **% Daily Value:** Total Fat 0g 0%; Saturated Fat 0g 0%; Cholesterol 0mg 0%; Sodium 0mg 0%; Total Carbohydrate 5g 2%; Dietary Fiber 0g 0%; Sugars 4g; Protein 0g; Vitamin A 0%; Vitamin C 2%; Calcium 0%; Iron 0% **Dietary Exchanges:** Free, 0 Carbohydrate Choice

salsa and black bean dip

Prep Time: 10 minutes

4 slices bacon, cooked, crumbled

½ cup chopped green onions

1 cup chunky-style salsa

1 (15-oz.) can black beans, drained

1. In medium bowl, combine all ingredients; mix well.

2. Cover; refrigerate 1 to 2 hours to blend flavors. Serve with tortilla chips.

Yield: 3 cups

NUTRITION INFORMATION PER SERVING
Serving Size: 1 Tablespoon; Calories 15; Calories from Fat 0 **% Daily Value:** Total Fat 0g 0%; Saturated Fat 0g 0%; Cholesterol 0mg 0%; Sodium 65mg 3%; Total Carbohydrate 3g 1%; Dietary Fiber 1g 4%; Sugars 0g; Protein 1g; Vitamin A 0%; Vitamin C 2%; Calcium 0%; Iron 2% **Dietary Exchanges:** Free, 0 Carbohydrate Choice

honey-sage whipped butter

Prep Time: 5 minutes

2 tablespoons finely chopped
fresh sage

2 tablespoons honey

½ cup butter, softened

1. In small microwave-safe bowl, combine chopped sage and honey; mix well. Microwave on High for 15 seconds. Cool 2 minutes.

2. Beat butter in small bowl with electric mixer at medium speed until fluffy. Add honey mixture; beat well. Store in refrigerator for up to 2 weeks or freeze for 1 month.

Yield: ½ cup

NUTRITION INFORMATION PER SERVING
Serving Size: 1 Tablespoon; Calories 120; Calories from Fat 110 **% Daily Value:** Total Fat 12g 18%; Saturated Fat 7g 35%; Cholesterol 30mg 10%; Sodium 75mg 3%; Total Carbohydrate 4g 1%; Dietary Fiber 0g 0%; Sugars 4g; Protein 0g; Vitamin A 8%; Vitamin C 0%; Calcium 0%; Iron 0% **Dietary Exchanges:** 2½ Fat, 0 Carbohydrate Choice

Special Touch
This makes a cute gift when paired with kitchen accessories in bee designs. Look for bee napkins, butter spreaders and appetizer plates at specialty and kitchen supply stores. Arrange the whole assortment in a basket.

kiddy pop ornaments

1. Attach assorted small candies to suckers
   with looped handles using vanilla frosting.
   Let stand until dry.

2. Place on tree using looped handles of
   suckers as hangers.

hot buttered rum sauce

Prep Time: 10 minutes

1 cup firmly packed brown sugar

½ cup butter

⅛ teaspoon salt

1 (14-oz.) can sweetened condensed milk (not evaporated)

¼ cup dark rum

2 teaspoons vanilla

1. In medium saucepan, combine brown sugar, butter, salt and condensed milk. Bring to a boil over medium heat, stirring constantly to prevent scorching. Cook until sugar is dissolved. Remove from heat.

2. Stir in rum and vanilla. Reheat sauce before serving. Store in refrigerator.

Yield: 2½ cups

NUTRITION INFORMATION PER SERVING
Serving Size: 1 Tablespoon; Calories 80; Calories from Fat 25 **% Daily Value:** Total Fat 3g 5%; Saturated Fat 2g 10%; Cholesterol 10mg 3%; Sodium 45mg 2%; Total Carbohydrate 11g 4%; Dietary Fiber 0g 0%; Sugars 11g; Protein 1g; Vitamin A 2%; Vitamin C 0%; Calcium 4%; Iron 0% **Dietary Exchanges:** ½ Fat, 1 Other Carbohydrate, 1 Carbohydrate Choice

cranberry mustard

Prep Time: 10 minutes

½ cup finely chopped sweetened dried cranberries

2 tablespoons honey

1 (8-oz.) jar Dijon mustard

1. In small microwave-safe bowl, combine cranberries, honey and 1 tablespoon of the mustard; mix well. Microwave on High for 45 to 60 seconds or until hot. Cool 2 minutes.

2. Add remaining mustard; mix well. Store in refrigerator for up to 1 month.

Yield: 1½ cups

NUTRITION INFORMATION PER SERVING
Serving Size: 1 Tablespoon; Calories 25; Calories from Fat 10 **% Daily Value:** Total Fat 1g 2%; Saturated Fat 0g 0%; Cholesterol 0mg 0%; Sodium 240mg 10%; Total Carbohydrate 4g 1%; Dietary Fiber 0g 0%; Sugars 3g; Protein 0g; Vitamin A 0%; Vitamin C 0%; Calcium 0%; Iron 0% **Dietary Exchanges:** Free, 0 Carbohydrate Choice

caramel pecan sauce

Prep Time: 15 minutes   (Ready in 30 minutes)

1 cup firmly packed brown sugar

½ cup chopped pecans

½ cup whipping cream

¼ cup light corn syrup

2 tablespoons butter or margarine

½ teaspoon vanilla

1. In medium saucepan, combine all ingredients except vanilla; mix well. Bring to a boil over medium heat, stirring occasionally. Boil 3 to 4 minutes, stirring occasionally. Remove from heat.

2. Stir in vanilla. Cool about 15 minutes or until thickened. Store in refrigerator.

Yield: 1⅓ cups

NUTRITION INFORMATION PER SERVING
Serving Size: 1 Tablespoon; Calories 80; Calories from Fat 35 **% Daily Value:** Total Fat 4g 6%; Saturated Fat 2g 10%; Cholesterol 8mg 3%; Sodium 15mg 1%; Total Carbohydrate 11g 4%; Dietary Fiber 0g 0%; Sugars 10g; Protein 0g; Vitamin A 2%; Vitamin C 0%; Calcium 0%; Iron 2% **Dietary Exchanges:** ½ Fat, 1 Other Carbohydrate, 1 Carbohydrate Choice

Substitution
Leave out the pecans in this sweet sauce and use walnuts or cashews instead if you like.

holiday spiced nuts

Prep Time: 30 minutes   (Ready in 50 minutes)

⅓ cup butter, cut into pieces

⅓ cup light corn syrup

1 teaspoon cardamom

1 teaspoon nutmeg

¼ teaspoon salt

1½ cups pecan halves

1 cup salted or unsalted whole cashews

⅓ cup blanched whole almonds

1. Heat oven to 375°F. Line 15×10×1-inch baking pan with heavy-duty foil. Place butter pieces in foil-lined pan. Place pan in oven for 4 to 5 minutes or until butter is melted.

2. Remove pan from oven. Add corn syrup, cardamom, nutmeg and salt; mix well. Add pecans, cashews and almonds; stir to coat. Spread in single layer in pan.

3. Bake at 375°F. for 10 to 15 minutes or until nuts are golden brown. Remove from oven; immediately stir mixture. Cool 20 minutes or until completely cooled. Store in tightly covered container.

Yield: 4 cups

NUTRITION INFORMATION PER SERVING
Serving Size: 2 Tablespoons; Calories 110; Calories from Fat 80 **% Daily Value:** Total Fat 9g 14%; Saturated Fat 2g 10%; Cholesterol 5mg 2%; Sodium 60mg 3%; Total Carbohydrate 5g 2%; Dietary Fiber 1g 4%; Sugars 2g; Protein 2g; Vitamin A 2%; Vitamin C 0%; Calcium 0%; Iron 2% **Dietary Exchanges:** 2 Fat, 0 Carbohydrate Choice

Special Touch

Holiday nuts are one of the easiest, most welcome kitchen gifts. Prepare an extra batch of this recipe to have ready for work, neighborhood and family parties. Package the nuts in holiday-themed cellophane bags tied with metallic ribbon.

9 *Kids'*
Workshop

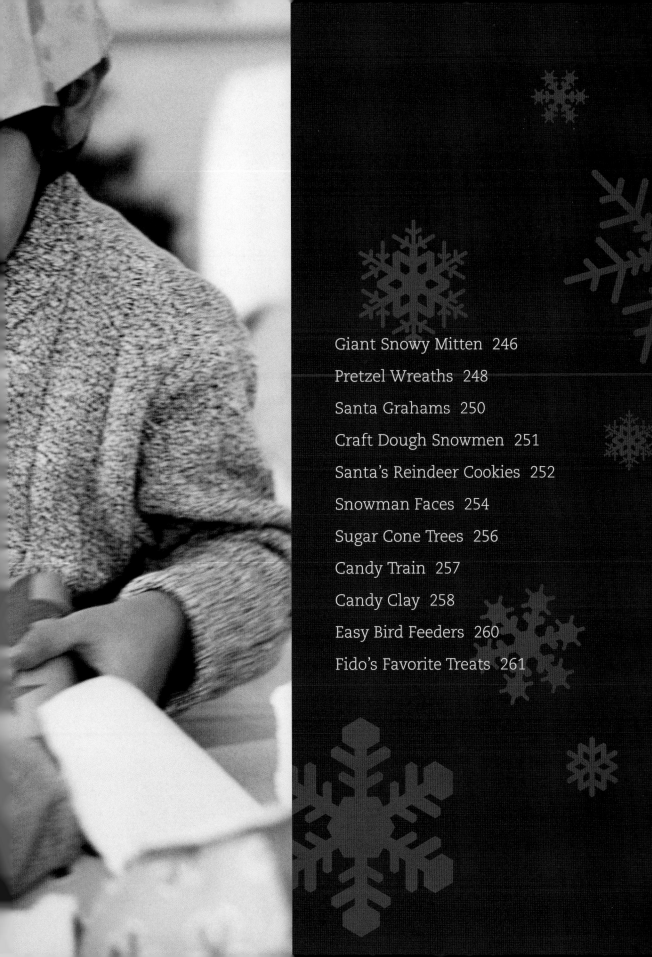

Giant Snowy Mitten 246

Pretzel Wreaths 248

Santa Grahams 250

Craft Dough Snowmen 251

Santa's Reindeer Cookies 252

Snowman Faces 254

Sugar Cone Trees 256

Candy Train 257

Candy Clay 258

Easy Bird Feeders 260

Fido's Favorite Treats 261

giant snowy mitten

Prep Time: 40 minutes   (Ready in 1 hour 10 minutes)

½ (18-oz.) roll refrigerated sugar cookie dough

1 cup vanilla ready-to-spread frosting (from 16-oz. can)

Green, red and blue food color

1. Place cookie dough in freezer for 30 minutes or until very firm.

2. Heat oven to 350°F. Line cookie sheet with parchment paper. Cut cookie dough into 16 slices. Arrange 15 slices, ¼ inch apart, in shape of mitten on paper-lined cookie sheet. (See diagram.) Roll remaining slice of dough into log; place on side of mitten. Flatten to form oblong shape for thumb.

3. Bake at 350°F. for 14 to 15 minutes or until golden brown. Remove parchment paper with cookie from cookie sheet. Cool 15 minutes or until completely cooled. Remove cookie from paper.

4. Meanwhile, reserve ½ cup frosting to spread over cookie. Divide remaining ½ cup frosting into thirds; place in 3 small bowls. Add different food color to each bowl; blend well. Place each colored frosting in small resealable food storage plastic bag. Cut small hole in bottom corner of each bag.

5. Spread reserved white frosting evenly over cooled cookie. Pipe colored frostings into decorative pattern on mitten. To serve, cut cookie into pieces.

Yield: 8 servings

NUTRITION INFORMATION PER SERVING
Serving Size: ⅛ of Recipe; Calories 300; Calories from Fat 90 **% Daily Value:** Total Fat 10g 15%; Saturated Fat 6g 30%; Cholesterol 5mg 2%; Sodium 110mg 5%; Total Carbohydrate 51g 17%; Dietary Fiber 0g 0%; Sugars 41g; Protein 1g; Vitamin A 0%; Vitamin C 0%; Calcium 2%; Iron 4% **Dietary Exchanges:** 2 Fat, 3½ Other Carbohydrates, 3½ Carbohydrate Choices

pretzel wreaths

Prep Time: 1 hour

6 oz. white vanilla chips, vanilla-flavored candy coating or almond bark, chopped

72 small pretzel twists (from 10-oz. pkg.)

6 (24-inch) pieces red string licorice

1. Line 2 cookie sheets with waxed paper. Melt vanilla chips in medium saucepan over low heat, stirring constantly.

2. To make each wreath, place 6 pretzels in circle on waxed-paper-lined cookie sheet, placing single holes of pretzels on outside of ring. Remove 1 pretzel from circle; dip inner section halfway into melted chips, coating inner (2-hole) section. Place dipped pretzel back into circle formation. Continue with remaining pretzels in circle.

3. To form top layer of wreath, dip 6 additional pretzels, one at a time, in coating as directed above. Place over first circle so that coated holes match holes underneath but overlap 2 pretzels. (Inner holes must remain open to weave licorice through.) Refrigerate wreaths 15 minutes or until coating is firm.

4. Weave 1 piece of string licorice through inner holes of each wreath. Tie bow with licorice ends.

Yield: 6 wreaths

NUTRITION INFORMATION PER SERVING
Serving Size: 1 Wreath; Calories 250; Calories from Fat 90 **% Daily Value:** Total Fat 10g 15%; Saturated Fat 6g 30%; Cholesterol 5mg 2%; Sodium 300mg 13%; Total Carbohydrate 37g 12%; Dietary Fiber 0g 0%; Sugars 23g; Protein 3g; Vitamin A 0%; Vitamin C 0%; Calcium 6%; Iron 4% **Dietary Exchanges:** 1 Starch, 2 Fat, 1½ Other Carbohydrates, 2½ Carbohydrate Choices

Special Touch
Older kids with steady hands can add "berries" to these edible ornaments by attaching red candy-coated chocolate candies to the wreaths with small drops of the melted vanilla chips. Younger children can sprinkle red-colored sprinkles over the top of the wreaths before the coating sets.

places, everyone!

Attach personalized holiday gift
tags to candy canes to designate
each seat at the table.

santa grahams

Prep Time: 30 minutes

1¼ cups vanilla ready-to-spread frosting (from 16-oz. can)

Red food color

12 (2½-inch-square) graham crackers

1 cup (about 75) miniature marshmallows, cut in half crosswise

6 small red gumdrops, cut in half crosswise

24 red cinnamon candies

1. Line cookie sheet with waxed paper. Place ¼ cup of the frosting in small bowl. Add ¼ teaspoon red food color; blend well for red color. Place remaining 1 cup frosting in another bowl. Add 1 drop red food color; blend well for pink color.

2. For each cookie, frost 1 inch of one corner of cracker with red frosting for Santa's hat. Place 1 marshmallow piece in corner for pom-pom.

3. Frost remainder of cracker with pink frosting. Place marshmallow pieces on pink frosting around 2 sides for beard. Add gumdrop for nose and cinnamon candies for eyes. Place on waxed-paper-lined cookie sheet. Let stand until frosting is set before storing.

Yield: 12 cookies

NUTRITION INFORMATION PER SERVING
Serving Size: 1 Cookie; Calories 195; Calories from Fat 55 **% Daily Value:** Total Fat 6g 9%; Saturated Fat 5g 25%; Cholesterol 0mg 0%; Sodium 45mg 2%; Total Carbohydrate 35g 12%; Dietary Fiber 0g 0%; Sugars 30g; Protein 0g; Vitamin A 0%; Vitamin C 0%; Calcium 0%; Iron 0% **Dietary Exchanges:** 1 Fat, 2½ Other Carbohydrates, 2 Carbohydrate Choices

craft dough snowmen

Prep Time: 30 minutes   (Ready in 1 hour 45 minutes)

2 cups all-purpose flour

1 cup salt

¾ cup water

Acrylic paint or polyurethane

1. Heat oven to 350°F. Grease large cookie sheet. In large bowl, combine flour and salt; mix well. Gradually add water, stirring until a stiff dough forms. If necessary, add up to ¼ cup additional water to moisten all dry ingredients. Knead dough 5 minutes or until smooth.

2. To make each snowman, shape one 2-inch ball of dough, one 1-inch ball of dough and two ¼-inch balls of dough. Place 2-inch ball on greased cookie sheet; moisten top edge of ball and place 1-inch ball on it, gently pressing balls together. Moisten 1 edge of each ¼-inch ball; gently press onto each side of 2-inch ball to resemble snowman arms.

3. Bake at 350°F. for 35 to 45 minutes or until firm to the touch. Turn oven off; let stand in warm oven for 2 hours to finish drying.

4. Spray or brush snowmen with assorted colors of acrylic paint or clear, glossy polyurethane. Let dry completely. Decorate as desired using scraps of fabric or ribbon for scarves. Attach hat and broom from craft store or glue felt circle on snowmen for hats. DO NOT EAT.

Yield: About 2 cups dough

Family Ties

Kids can also roll out and cut this multiuse craft dough with their favorite cookie cutters. For colored dough, add a few drops of food color to portions of the dough and knead to blend.

santa's reindeer cookies

Prep Time: 1 hour

1 (18-oz.) roll refrigerated sugar cookie dough, well chilled

4 tablespoons all-purpose flour

⅓ cup vanilla ready-to-spread frosting (from 16-oz. can)

4 cups (108) small pretzel twists

14 candied red or green cherries, cut into quarters, or spice drop candies

⅓ cup raisins

1. Heat oven to 350°F. Cut cookie dough in half; unwrap one half and refrigerate remaining half of dough until needed. Coat sides of dough with 2 tablespoons of the flour.

2. Roll out dough to form 9-inch square, using additional flour as needed to prevent sticking. Cut square into four 2¼-inch-wide strips; cut each strip into 6 equal triangles. Place on ungreased cookie sheet.

3. Bake at 350°F. for 6 to 8 minutes or until light golden brown. Cool 1 minute; remove from cookie sheet. Cool 10 minutes or until completely cooled. Repeat with remaining half of dough and flour.

4. Spread frosting over cookies. Press pretzels into top 2 corners of each cookie to resemble antlers. Place cherry piece at bottom to resemble nose. Place raisins on frosting for eyes. Let stand until frosting is set before storing.

Yield: 4 dozen cookies

NUTRITION INFORMATION PER SERVING
Serving Size: 1 Cookie; Calories 130; Calories from Fat 35 **% Daily Value:** Total Fat 4g 6%; Saturated Fat 3g 15%; Cholesterol 0mg 0%; Sodium 230mg 10%; Total Carbohydrate 22g 7%; Dietary Fiber 1g 4%; Sugars 10g; Protein 2g; Vitamin A 0%; Vitamin C 0%; Calcium 0%; Iron 4% **Dietary Exchanges:** 1 Starch, 1 Fat, ½ Other Carbohydrate, 1½ Carbohydrate Choices

Substitution
Chocolate ready-to-spread frosting can be used in place of the vanilla frosting, and chocolate chips or white vanilla chips can be used instead of the raisins. Or mix and match so each cookie has a unique look.

snowman faces

Prep Time: 35 minutes

1 cup vanilla ready-to-spread frosting (from 16-oz. can)

3 oz. vanilla-flavored candy coating or almond bark, chopped

20 creme-filled vanilla or chocolate sandwich cookies

1 tablespoon miniature semisweet chocolate chips

10 small gumdrops

2 orange slice jelly candies, flattened slightly

Red decorating gel

1. Line cookie sheets with waxed paper. In small saucepan, combine ¾ cup of the frosting and the candy coating. Melt over low heat, stirring occasionally until smooth. Remove from heat.

2. With tongs, dip each cookie in melted frosting mixture, coating completely. Lay cookies flat on waxed-paper-lined cookie sheet. Let stand about 10 minutes or until set.

3. Meanwhile, place remaining ¼ cup frosting in small resealable food storage plastic bag. Cut tiny hole in bottom corner of bag.

4. On each sandwich cookie, use small amount of frosting to attach chocolate chips for eyes. Cut each gumdrop in half; frost cut sides and attach to sides of cookie to resemble earmuffs.

5. Attach small wedge cut from slightly flattened jelly candy for nose. Draw mouth with red decorating gel. Let stand until frosting is set before storing.

Yield: 20 cookies

Family Ties

This is a great recipe to spark young imaginations. Have all the chocolate chips, gumdrops, jelly candies and decorating gel ready, and let the kids decide how the snowman faces should look.

sugar cone trees

Prep Time: 20 minutes   (Ready in 1 hour 20 minutes)

Green food color, if desired

1 (16-oz.) can vanilla ready-to-spread frosting

8 flat-bottom ice cream cones

8 sugar cones

Assorted small candies

1. Stir green food color into frosting until well blended. Frost top rim of flat-bottom cones.

2. To form each tree shape, place open end of 1 sugar cone over frosted rim of 1 flat-bottom cone, standing each on flat end. Let stand 1 hour or until frosting is firm.

3. Frost outer surface of sugar cones with green frosting. Decorate as desired with candies.

Yield: 8 trees

NUTRITION INFORMATION PER SERVING
Serving Size: 1 Tree; Calories 335; Calories from Fat 80 **% Daily Value:** Total Fat 9g 14%; Saturated Fat 8g 40%; Cholesterol 5mg 2%; Sodium 25mg 1%; Total Carbohydrate 62g 21%; Dietary Fiber 0g 0%; Sugars 49g; Protein 1g; Vitamin A 0%; Vitamin C 0%; Calcium 0%; Iron 2% **Dietary Exchanges:** 2 Fat, 4 Other Carbohydrates, 4 Carbohydrate Choices

candy train

Prep Time: 1 hour

1 candy bar miniature,
unwrapped

4 fun-sized candy bars,
unwrapped

Chocolate ready-to-spread
frosting (from 16-oz. can)

4 bite-sized creme-filled
sandwich cookies, separated

4 red gumdrops

1 frilly topped toothpick

8 bite-sized round buttery
crackers

Assorted small candies or
pretzel sticks

1. For train engine, attach candy bar miniature to top of fun-sized candy bar with frosting. Attach cookie halves to sides for wheels. To form smokestack, attach gumdrop, wide end up, to top with toothpick.

2. For coal car, attach crackers with frosting to sides of fun-size candy bar for wheels. With frosting, attach small candies for coal.

3. For log car, attach cookie halves with frosting to sides of fun-sized candy bar for wheels. With frosting, attach pretzel sticks for logs.

4. For caboose, attach crackers with frosting to sides of fun-sized candy bars for wheels. With frosting, stack gumdrops on top.

5. Let stand until frosting is set.

Yield: 1 candy train

Family Ties
Let kids have fun making a candy train for each guest at the dinner party. Show the kids how to draw railroad tracks for the trains on paper place mats along the edges.

candy clay

Prep Time: 15 minutes   (Ready in 1 hour 45 minutes)

10 oz. vanilla-flavored candy coating or almond bark, cut into pieces

⅓ cup light corn syrup

4 food colors

2 teaspoons assorted small candies

1. Line 8-inch square pan with foil; spray foil with nonstick cooking spray. Place candy coating in medium microwave-safe bowl. Microwave on High for 1 minute. Stir; continue to microwave in 15-second increments until coating can be stirred smooth.

2. Add corn syrup; blend well. Spread candy-coating mixture evenly in sprayed foil-lined pan. Let stand at room temperature for 20 to 60 minutes or until dough is firm enough to handle.

3. Spray inside of 4 food storage plastic bags with nonstick cooking spray. Divide dough into 4 sections. Squeeze each section with hands until workable. To color each section, place dough in sprayed bag. Add food color as desired (about ⅛ teaspoon for ¼ of dough); knead dough until color is well blended. Turn bag inside out; scrape out dough. Let stand 15 to 30 minutes before sculpting.

4. Cut each section of clay into 3 pieces. Sculpt clay as desired. Decorate with small candies. Candy clay will harden when exposed to air. (Store unused clay in sealed plastic bag. Before sculpting, knead with hands to soften or microwave several seconds.)

Yield: 12 candies

NUTRITION INFORMATION PER SERVING
Serving Size: 1 Candy; Calories 165; Calories from Fat 70 **% Daily Value:** Total Fat 8g 12%; Saturated Fat 5g 25%; Cholesterol 5mg 2%; Sodium 35mg 1%; Total Carbohydrate 22g 7%; Dietary Fiber 0g 0%; Sugars 19g; Protein 1g; Vitamin A 0%; Vitamin C 0%; Calcium 4%; Iron 0% **Dietary Exchanges:** ½ Starch, 2 Fat, ½ Other Carbohydrate, 1 Carbohydrate Choice

Special Touch
Try rolling the dough in edible glitter or decorative sugar. Not only does it make the dough easier to shape, but it also adds a festive touch.

easy bird feeders

Prep Time: 20 minutes   (Ready in 2 hours 15 minutes)

1 lb. chopped suet

1 cup wild bird seed

1 cup raw sunflower seeds or wild bird seed

3 oranges, cut in half, pulp removed

String

1. Melt suet in large saucepan over low heat, stirring occasionally. Stir in bird seed and sunflower seeds. Cool 15 to 20 minutes. Refrigerate 30 to 45 minutes or until mixture starts to set but is not solid.

2. Meanwhile, with point of small knife, punch 2 holes opposite each other in each orange half, ½ inch down from cut edge. Cut 6 pieces of string to desired length for hanging. Push ends of 1 string through holes, from outside to inside, in 1 orange half; tie each end in a knot.

3. Place each orange half in small bowl or place orange halves in baking pan. Spoon suet mixture into each orange half, pressing in gently and mounding in center. Refrigerate 1 hour or until firm. Hang outdoors. DO NOT EAT.

Yield: 6 feeders

Family Ties

Check out books from the library on birds, polish the lens on the binoculars and go bird-watching right in your own backyard. Research what kinds of birds can be found in your area, and keep a checklist of which birds you see.

fido's favorite treats

Prep Time: 20 minutes   (Ready in 1 hour 20 minutes)

1 cup rolled oats

⅓ cup butter or margarine

1 cup boiling water

¾ cup cornmeal

1 tablespoon sugar

1 to 2 teaspoons chicken or beef-flavored instant bouillon

½ cup milk

4 oz. (1 cup) shredded Cheddar cheese

1 egg, beaten

2 to 3 cups all-purpose or whole wheat flour

1. Heat oven to 325°F. Grease cookie sheets. In large bowl, combine rolled oats, butter and boiling water; mix well. Let stand 10 minutes.

2. Stir in cornmeal, sugar, bouillon, milk, cheese and egg; mix well. Add flour 1 cup at a time, mixing well after each addition to form a stiff dough.

3. On floured surface, knead in remaining flour until dough is smooth and no longer sticky, 3 to 4 minutes. Roll or pat dough to ½-inch thickness. Cut with bone-shaped cookie cutter; place 1 inch apart on greased cookie sheets.

4. Bake at 325°F. for 35 to 45 minutes or until golden brown. Remove from cookie sheets. Cool 15 minutes or until completely cooled. Store in loosely covered container.

Yield: 3½ dozen large or 8 dozen small dog biscuits

Special Touch

Give a package of these canine treats to your favorite dog. Include a bone-shaped cutter and a copy of the recipe for the dog owner.

Helpful Nutrition and Cooking Information

Nutrition Guidelines

The nutrition information can help you estimate how specific recipes contribute to your overall meal plan. The nutrition information with each recipe includes calories, fat, cholesterol, sodium, carbohydrate, dietary fiber, sugars, protein, vitamins A and C, calcium and iron.

Each recipe also lists Percent Daily Values (% DVs). The % DVs tell you how much the nutrients in one serving contribute to a 2,000-calorie diet. For example, if the DV for total fat is 10%, this means one serving of this food contributes 10% of the total fat suggested for a person on 2,000 calories per day.

We also included dietary exchanges for those of you who prefer this nutritional "accounting" method over traditional calorie watching. If you are following a medically prescribed diet, consult your physician or registered dietitian about this nutrition information.

Recommended Intake for a Daily Diet of 2,000 Calories As Set by the Food and Drug Administration

Total Fat	Less than 65g
Saturated Fat	Less than 20g
Cholesterol	Less than 300mg
Sodium	Less than 2,400mg
Total Carbohydrate	300g
Dietary Fiber	25g

CRITERIA USED FOR CALCULATING NUTRITION

The first ingredient was used wherever a choice is given (such as ⅓ cup sour cream or plain yogurt).

The larger ingredient amount was used wherever a range is given (such as 3- to 3½-lb. cut-up broiler-fryer chicken).

The first serving number was used wherever a range is given (such as 4 to 6 servings).

"If desired" ingredients are not included, whether mentioned in the ingredient list or in the recipe directions as a suggestion (such as "Sprinkle with brown sugar, if desired").

Only the amount of a marinade or frying oil that is estimated to be absorbed by the food during preparation or cooking was calculated.

INGREDIENTS USED IN RECIPE TESTING AND NUTRITION CALCULATIONS

Ingredients used for testing represent those that the majority of consumers use in their homes: large eggs, 2% milk, 80%-lean ground beef, canned chicken broth and vegetable oil spread containing not less than 65% fat.

Fat-free, low-fat or low-sodium products were not used, unless otherwise indicated.

Solid vegetable shortening (not butter, margarine, nonstick cooking sprays or vegetable oil spread, as they can cause sticking problems) was used to grease pans, unless otherwise indicated.

EQUIPMENT USED IN RECIPE TESTING

We use equipment for testing that the majority of consumers use in their homes. If a specific piece of equipment (such as a wire whisk) is necessary for recipe success, it will be listed in the recipe.

Cookware and bakeware without nonstick coatings were used, unless otherwise indicated.

No dark-colored, black or insulated bakeware was used.

When a pan is specified in a recipe, a metal pan was used; a baking dish or glass pie pan means ovenproof glass was used.

An electric hand mixer was used for mixing only when mixer speeds are specified in the recipe directions. When a mixer speed is not given, a spoon or fork was used.

Determining Preparation Times

The "Prep Time: minutes" at the beginning of each recipe serves as a guide for the time needed to make a recipe. The "Prep Time" is the active "hands on" preparation time. Whenever possible, active prep time is done simultaneously with other steps. The "(Ready in minutes/hours)" notation is added when a recipe requires additional time beyond the active prep time. For example, the "Ready in" time includes the active prep time plus marinating, cooking, baking or grilling times as well as cooling, refrigerating or freezing times.

In establishing these times, the following specifics also have been used:

❋ The longest time in a cooking/baking range
❋ The shortest time for marinating ingredients
❋ No time is counted for heating the oven or grill
❋ The times listed are for the first cooking method
   if two methods are provided

Index

Note: Pages in italics refer to photographs.

A

Aïoli, Chile, 34, 35
Aïoli Dip, 74, 75
Almond(s)
  Baby Carrots, 142, 143
  Crescent Ring, Danish, 66
  Holiday Focaccia, 63
  Holiday Spiced Nuts, 242, 243
  Spiced Chocolate Crinkles, 202
Angel Cake, Christmas, 168–69
Appetizers. See Starters and snacks
Apple(s)
  -Cranberry Streusel Pie, 174, 175
  -Ginger Scones, 52, 53
  -Glazed Pork Chops with Sage-
    Apple Stuffing, 123
  and Onions, Sweet Potatoes
    with, 147
  Spiced Cider Cheesecake, 188–89
  Winter Fruit Salad, 159
Apricots, Marzipan-Stuffed, in
  Chocolate, 228
Asian Crab Mini Quiches, 32

B

Bacon
  Beef, and Barley Soup, 80
  Chicken Peanut Kabobs, 28, 29
  Make-Ahead Scrambled Eggs,
    83
Bagel 'n Brie Brunch Strata, 137
Barley, Beef and Bacon Soup, 80
Bars
  Caramel Candy, 214, 215
  Chocolate-Covered Cheesecake
    Bites, 212
  Chocolate-Toffee, 207
  White Chocolate-Raspberry, 208,
    209
Bean(s)
  Black, and Salsa Dip, 236, 236
  Black, -Chipotle Chili, 103

Green, Parmesan-Garlic Butter,
    145, 145
  Mediterranean Fennel Salad, 156,
    157
  Oven-Roasted Pork Chops and
    Vegetables, 78, 79
Beef
  Bacon, and Barley Soup, 80
  Burgundy, Slow-Cooked, 73
  Chili Cheese Dip and Potato
    Wedges, 20, 20
  Creole Meatballs, 21
  Crostini with Caper Mayonnaise,
    18
  Fondue and Dipping Sauces, 74,
    75
  Pepper-Crusted Prime Rib with
    Zinfandel Sauce, 112, 113
  Peppered Steak with Brandy-
    Mushroom Sauce, 109
  Prime Rib-Eye Roast, 114
  Spinach Pesto Manicotti, 76
  Steak Neapolitan, 110, 110
  Tenderloin, Peppered, with Wine
    Sauce, 111
  Tenderloin and Caramelized
    Onion Sandwiches, 22
Bird Feeders, Easy, 260
Biscuits, Crispy Onion, 58
Brandied Cranberries, Baked, 163
Brandy-Mushroom Sauce,
  Peppered Steak with, 109
Bread(s). See also Sandwiches,
  bite-sized
  Apple-Ginger Scones, 52, 53
  Bagel 'n Brie Brunch Strata, 137
  Cranberry Upside-Down Muffins,
    48, 49
  Crispy Onion Biscuits, 58
  Danish Almond Crescent Ring,
    66
  Dill-Parmesan Popovers, 55
  Double-Chocolate Batter, 59
  Dried Cherry–Cardamom, 60,
    61

Holiday Focaccia, 63
  Merry Ginger Muffin Mix, 232,
    233
  Onion-Garlic Loaf, 62
  Overnight Caramel-Apple Rolls,
    56, 57
  Parmesan-Herb Muffins, 50
  Pudding, Eggnog, with Cherry-
    Bourbon Sauce, 193
  Savory Cheese and Scallion
    Scones, 54
  Savory Nutty Crescents, 46
  Sweet Nutcracker Braid, 68, 69
  Three-Cheese Crescent
    Pinwheels, 47
  Turkey and Ham Crescent Braid,
    94, 95
  White Chocolate-Iced Cranberry,
    64, 65
Breakfast and brunch dishes
  Apple-Ginger Scones, 52, 53
  Bagel 'n Brie Brunch Strata, 137
  Cranberry Upside-Down Muffins,
    48, 49
  Danish Almond Crescent Ring,
    66
  Double-Chocolate Batter Bread,
    59
  Dried Cherry-Cardamom Bread,
    60, 61
  Holiday Focaccia, 63
  Make-Ahead Scrambled Eggs, 83
  Overnight Caramel-Apple Rolls,
    56, 57
  Sausage and Egg Brunch Bake, 82
  Seafood and Cheese Brunch
    Bake, 100, 101
  Sweet Nutcracker Braid, 68, 69
  White Chocolate-Iced Cranberry
    Bread, 64, 65
Brittle, Spiced Walnut, 218
Broccoli
  Turkey and Ham Crescent Braid,
    94, 95
  with Walnut-Garlic Butter, 140

Brownie Dessert, Creamy Peppermint-Topped, 194, 195
Brussels Sprouts, Honey-Mustard Dilled, 141
Buckeyes, Almost-Instant, 222, 223
Butter, Honey-Sage Whipped, 237
Buttered Rum Sauce, Hot, 239, 239

C
Cabbage
    Festive Coleslaw with Citrus Vinaigrette, 162
Caffé Latte Crème Brûlée, 196
Cake
    Chocolate-Almond Mousse, 166, 167
    Chocolate-Cherry Cheesecake, 186, 187
    Christmas Angel, 168–69
    Cranberry, Quick Saucy, 170, 171
    Dark Gingerbread Bundt, 172
    Holiday Cherry-Chocolate, 173
    Mocha Truffle Cheesecake, 190, 191
    Spiced Cider Cheesecake, 188–89
Candy
    Almost-Instant Buckeyes, 222, 223
    Christmas Tree Candy Pops, 224, 225
    Cranberry-Walnut White Fudge, 219
    Layered Mint-Chocolate Fudge, 216, 217
    Marzipan-Stuffed Apricots in Chocolate, 228
    Peppermint-Bark Hearts, 220, 221
    Pretzel Wreaths, 248, 249
    Spiced Walnut Brittle, 218
    Sugar Cone Trees, 256, 256
Candy Clay, 258, 259
Candy Train, 257
Caramel-Apple Rolls, Overnight, 56, 57
Caramel Candy Bars, 214, 215
Caramel Pecan Sauce, 241
Cardamom Sandwich Cookies, 204, 205
Carrots
    Baby, Almond, 142, 143
    Beef, Bacon and Barley Soup, 80
    Oven-Roasted Pork Chops and Vegetables, 78, 79
    Skillet Chicken and Winter Vegetables, 90, 91

Slow-Cooked Beef Burgundy, 73
Cashew(s)
    -Chocolate Pie, 176
    Holiday Spiced Nuts, 242, 243
Cheese
    Bagel 'n Brie Brunch Strata, 137
    Chili Dip and Potato Wedges, 20, 20
    Chocolate-Cherry Cheesecake, 186, 187
    Chocolate-Covered Cheesecake Bites, 212
    Creamy Chicken-Vegetable Chowder, 86
    Dill-Parmesan Popovers, 55
    Goat, and Olive Phyllo Purses, 42
    Make-Ahead Scrambled Eggs, 83
    Mini Pizzas, 38
    Mocha Truffle Cheesecake, 190, 191
    Overnight Chicken Enchilada Bake, 93
    Parmesan-Garlic Butter Green Beans, 145, 145
    Parmesan-Herb Muffins, 50
    Pizza Lasagna, 84, 85
    Sausage and Egg Brunch Bake, 82
    and Scallion Scones, Savory, 54
    and Seafood Brunch Bake, 100, 101
    Smoky, and Potato Bake, 151
    Spiced Cider Cheesecake, 188–89
    Spinach Pesto Manicotti, 76
    Spread, Cherry-, 40, 41
    Three-, Crescent Pinwheels, 47
    Three-Potato Gratin, 148, 149
    Turkey and Ham Crescent Braid, 94, 95
    Turkey-Cranberry Quesadillas, 27
Cheesecake
    Bites, Chocolate-Covered, 212
    Chocolate-Cherry, 186, 187
    Mocha Truffle, 190, 191
    Spiced Cider, 188–89
Cherry(ies)
    -Balsamic Cornish Hen with Rice, 130, 131
    -Bourbon Sauce, Eggnog Bread Pudding with, 193
    -Cheese Spread, 40, 41
    -Chocolate Cake, Holiday, 173
    -Chocolate Cheesecake, 186, 187
    Cookies, Chocolate-Covered, 203
    Dried, -Cardamom Bread, 60, 61
    Holiday Focaccia, 63

Chestnut-Prune Stuffing, Roast Goose with, 132
Chicken
    Cacciatore, Party, 88, 89
    Enchilada Bake, Overnight, 93
    Newburg, Crescent, 92
    Peanut Kabobs, 28, 29
    and Sausage Stew, 87
    and Squash, Honey-Mustard Roasted, 126, 127
    -Vegetable Chowder, Creamy, 86
    and Winter Vegetables, Skillet, 90, 91
Chile Aïoli, 34, 35
Chili, Chipotle-Black Bean, 103
Chili Cheese Dip and Potato Wedges, 20, 20
Chipotle-Black Bean Chili, 103
Chocolate
    -Almond Mousse Cake, 166, 167
    -Cashew Pie, 176
    -Cherry Cake, Holiday, 173
    -Cherry Cheesecake, 186, 187
    -Covered Cheesecake Bites, 212
    -Covered Cherry Cookies, 203
    Creamy Peppermint-Topped Brownie Dessert, 194, 195
    Crinkles, Spiced, 202
    Double-, Batter Bread, 59
    Marzipan-Stuffed Apricots in, 228
    -Mint Fudge, Layered, 216, 217
    Mocha Truffle Cheesecake, 190, 191
    Spritz Cookies (var.), 206
    Strawberry-Fudge Pie, 177
    -Toffee Bars, 207
    Treats, Crispy, 229
    Triple-, Truffle Trees, 178, 179
    White, -Iced Cranberry Bread, 64, 65
    White, -Raspberry Bars, 208, 209
Chowder, Creamy Chicken-Vegetable, 86
Chutney, Spiced Pear, 235
Cider Cheesecake, Spiced, 188–89
Cilantro-Lime Shrimp with Chile Aïoli, 34, 35
Clay, Candy, 258, 259
Coffee
    Caffé Latte Crème Brûlée, 196
    Mix, Orange-Spice, 234
    Mocha Truffle Cheesecake, 190, 191

Coleslaw, Festive, with Citrus Vinaigrette, 162
Cookie Cutter Gifts, White Fudge, 230, 231
Cookies
 Caramel Candy Bars, 214, 215
 Cardamom Sandwich, 204, 205
 Chocolate-Covered Cheesecake Bites, 212
 Chocolate-Covered Cherry, 203
 Chocolate Spritz (var.), 206
 Chocolate-Toffee Bars, 207
 Christmas Cutouts, 200, 201
 Crispy Chocolate Treats, 229
 Giant Snowy Mitten, 246, 247
 Mint-Kissed Meringues, 210, 211
 Orange Spritz, 206
 Santa Grahams, 250, 250
 Santa's Reindeer, 252, 253
 Snowman Faces, 254, 255
 Spiced Chocolate Crinkles, 202
 White Chocolate-Raspberry Bars, 208, 209
Corn
 Beef, Bacon and Barley Soup, 80
 Creamy Chicken-Vegetable Chowder, 86
Cornbread-Cranberry Stuffing, Glazed Crown Roast with, 118, 119
Cornish Hen, Cherry-Balsamic, with Rice, 130, 131
Crab
 Mini Quiches, Asian, 32
 Seafood and Cheese Brunch Bake, 100, 101
 Teriyaki Seafood-Stuffed Mushrooms, 30, 31
Craft Dough Snowmen, 251
Cranberry(ies)
 -Apple Streusel Pie, 174, 175
 Baked Brandied, 163
 Bread, White Chocolate-Iced, 64, 65
 Cake, Quick Saucy, 170, 171
 -Cornbread Stuffing, Glazed Crown Roast with, 118, 119
 Mousse, 197
 Mustard, 240, 240
 -Peach Gingerbread Trifle, 192
 Sauce, Ruby, Crème Dessert with, 182
 Sauce, Zesty, Baked Ham with, 116

-Turkey Quesadillas, 27
Upside-Down Muffins, 48, 49
-Walnut White Fudge, 219
Crème Brûlée, Caffé Latte, 196
Creole Meatballs, 21
Crescent Braid, Turkey and Ham, 94, 95
Crescent Chicken Newburg, 92
Crescent Pinwheels, Three-Cheese, 47
Crescent Ring, Danish Almond, 66
Crescents, Savory Nutty, 46
Crostini, Beef, with Caper Mayonnaise, 18
Crostini, Pork Tenderloin, 24, 25
Curry Dip, 74, 75

D
Danish Almond Crescent Ring, 66
Dates
 Sweet Nutcracker Braid, 68, 69
 Winter Fruit Salad, 159
Desserts. See also Candy; Cookies
 Caffé Latte Crème Brûlée, 196
 Caramel Pecan Sauce, 241
 Chocolate-Almond Mousse Cake, 166, 167
 Chocolate-Cashew Pie, 176
 Chocolate-Cherry Cheesecake, 186, 187
 Christmas Angel Cake, 168–69
 Cranberry-Apple Streusel Pie, 174, 175
 Cranberry Mousse, 197
 Cranberry-Peach Gingerbread Trifle, 192
 Creamy Peppermint-Topped Brownie Dessert, 194, 195
 Dark Gingerbread Bundt Cake, 172
 Eggnog Bread Pudding with Cherry-Bourbon Sauce, 193
 Eggnog Ice Cream Dessert, 184
 Holiday Cherry-Chocolate Cake, 173
 Hot Buttered Rum Sauce, 239, 239
 Individual Lemon-Lime Cream Tarts, 180, 180
 Mocha Truffle Cheesecake, 190, 191
 Orange Crème Dessert with Ruby Cranberry Sauce, 182
 Pomegranate Tartlets, 181

Quick Saucy Cranberry Cake, 170, 171
Raspberry Cream Heart, 185
Spiced Cider Cheesecake, 188–89
Strawberry-Fudge Pie, 177
Triple-Chocolate Truffle Trees, 178, 179
Deviled Lobster Tails, 134, 135
Dill-Parmesan Popovers, 55
Dipping sauce
 Aïoli Dip, 74, 75
 Curry Dip, 74, 75
 Horseradish Sauce, 74, 75
 Steak Sauce, 74, 75
Dips
 Chili Cheese, and Potato Wedges, 20, 20
 Salsa and Black Bean, 236, 236
Dog biscuits
 Fido's Favorite Treats, 261
Dough Snowmen, Craft, 251

E
Eggnog Bread Pudding with Cherry-Bourbon Sauce, 193
Eggnog Ice Cream Dessert, 184
Eggplant
 Winter Portobello Ratatouille, 105
Egg(s)
 Bagel 'n Brie Brunch Strata, 137
 and Sausage Brunch Bake, 82
 Scrambled, Make-Ahead, 83
 Seafood and Cheese Brunch Bake, 100, 101
Endive, Smoked Salmon on, 33
Entrées, casual
 Beef, Bacon and Barley Soup, 80
 Beef Fondue and Dipping Sauces, 74, 75
 Chicken and Sausage Stew, 87
 Chipotle-Black Bean Chili, 103
 Creamy Chicken-Vegetable Chowder, 86
 Crescent Chicken Newburg, 92
 Festive Oyster Stew, 102
 Herbed Alfredo Sauce over Linguine, 104, 104
 Lemon and Herb-Roasted Turkey Breast, 96, 97
 Make-Ahead Scrambled Eggs, 83
 menu ideas for, 72
 Oven-Roasted Pork Chops and Vegetables, 78, 79

Overnight Chicken Enchilada
  Bake, 93
Party Chicken Cacciatore, 88, 89
Pizza Lasagna, 84, 85
Sausage and Egg Brunch Bake,
  82
Seafood and Cheese Brunch
  Bake, 100, 101
Skillet Chicken and Winter
  Vegetables, 90, 91
Slow-Cooked Beef Burgundy, 73
Spinach Pesto Manicotti, 76
Turkey and Ham Crescent Braid,
  94, 95
Turkey with Italian Roasted
  Vegetables, 98
Winter Portobello Ratatouille,
  105
Entrées, Christmas Day
Apple-Glazed Pork Chops with
  Sage-Apple Stuffing, 123
Bagel 'n Brie Brunch Strata, 137
Baked Ham with Zesty
  Cranberry Sauce, 116
Cherry-Balsamic Cornish Hen
  with Rice, 130, 131
Deviled Lobster Tails, 134, 135
Fennel-Garlic Pork Roast, 122
Glazed Crown Roast with
  Cranberry-Cornbread Stuffing,
  118, 119
Honey-Mustard Roasted Chicken
  and Squash, 126, 127
Italian Roasted Salmon, 136
menu ideas for, 108
Pepper-Crusted Prime Rib with
  Zinfandel Sauce, 112, 113
Peppered Beef Tenderloin with
  Wine Sauce, 111
Peppered Steak with Brandy-
  Mushroom Sauce, 109
Pesto and Pepper-Stuffed Leg of
  Lamb, 124, 125
Pineapple-Orange Glazed Ham,
  117
Prime Rib-Eye Roast, 114
Roasted Orange-Fennel Halibut
  with Dijon Sauce, 133, 133
Roast Goose with Chestnut-
  Prune Stuffing, 132
Spice and Herb-Roasted Pork
  Tenderloin, 120, 121
Steak Neapolitan, 110, 110
Stuffed Roast Turkey and Gravy,
  128–29

F
Fennel-Garlic Pork Roast, 122
Fennel Salad, Mediterranean, 156,
  157
Fido's Favorite Treats, 261
Fish
  Italian Roasted Salmon, 136
  Roasted Orange-Fennel Halibut
    with Dijon Sauce, 133, 133
  Smoked Salmon on Endive, 33
Focaccia, Holiday, 63
Fondue, Beef, and Dipping Sauces,
  74, 75
Fruit. See also specific fruits
  Holiday Focaccia, 63
  Salad, Winter, 159
Fudge, Layered Mint-Chocolate,
  216, 217
Fudge, White, Cookie Cutter Gifts,
  230, 231
Fudge, White, Cranberry-Walnut,
  219

G
Garlic Smashed Red Potatoes, 153,
  153
Gift-giving ideas
  buttons and bow wrapping
    paper, 99, 99
  candy cane heart ornaments,
    183, 183
  gift basket ideas, 39, 39
  holiday sticker gift box, 189,
    189
  kiddy pop ornaments, 238, 238
  personal stamp for wrapping
    paper, 144, 144
  pet's paw gift box, 115, 115
  pretzel and candy garland, 81, 81
  stained-glass gift bag, 67, 67
Gifts from the Kitchen
  Caramel Pecan Sauce, 241
  Cranberry Mustard, 240, 240
  Crispy Chocolate Treats in a Jar,
    229
  Holiday Spiced Nuts, 242, 243
  Honey-Sage Whipped Butter,
    237
  Hot Buttered Rum Sauce, 239,
    239
  Marzipan-Stuffed Apricots in
    Chocolate, 228
  Merry Ginger Muffin Mix, 232,
    233
  Orange-Spice Coffee Mix, 234

Salsa and Black Bean Dip, 236,
  236
Spiced Pear Chutney, 235
White Fudge Cookie Cutter Gifts,
  230, 231
Gingerbread Bundt Cake, Dark, 172
Gingerbread Trifle, Cranberry-
  Peach, 192
Ginger Muffin Mix, Merry, 232, 233
Goat Cheese and Olive Phyllo
  Purses, 42
Goose, Roast, with Chestnut-Prune
  Stuffing, 132
Grahams, Santa, 250, 250
Gratin, Three-Potato, 148, 149
Green Beans
  Mediterranean Fennel Salad, 156,
    157
  Oven-Roasted Pork Chops and
    Vegetables, 78, 79
  Parmesan-Garlic Butter, 145, 145
Greens
  Mixed, Italian Salad, 110, 155
  Spinach Pesto Manicotti, 76
  Winter, with Pomegranate-
    Champagne Vinaigrette, 158

H
Halibut, Roasted Orange-Fennel,
  with Dijon Sauce, 133, 133
Ham, Baked, with Zesty Cranberry
  Sauce, 116
Ham, Pineapple-Orange Glazed,
  117
Ham and Turkey Crescent Braid,
  94, 95
Herbed Alfredo Sauce over
  Linguine, 104, 104
Herbed Polenta Stars, Baked, 154
Honey-Mustard Dilled Brussels
  Sprouts, 141
Honey-Mustard Roasted Chicken
  and Squash, 126, 127
Honey-Sage Whipped Butter, 237
Hors d'oeuvres. See Starters and
  snacks
Horseradish Sauce, 74, 75

I
Ice Cream Dessert, Eggnog, 184
Italian Mixed Green Salad, 110, 155
Italian Roasted Salmon, 136

J
Jiggle Bell Salad, 160, 161

K

Kabobs, Chicken Peanut, 28, 29
Kids' Workshop
　Candy Clay, 258, 259
　Candy Train, 257
　Craft Dough Snowmen, 251
　Easy Bird Feeders, 260
　Fido's Favorite Treats, 261
　Giant Snowy Mitten, 246, 247
　Pretzel Wreaths, 248, 249
　Santa Grahams, 250, 250
　Santa's Reindeer Cookies, 252,
　　253
　Snowman Faces, 254, 255
　Sugar Cone Trees, 256, 256

L

Lamb, Leg of, Pesto and Pepper-
　Stuffed, 124, 125
Lasagna, Pizza, 84, 85
Lemon and Herb-Roasted Turkey
　Breast, 96, 97
Lemon-Lime Cream Tarts,
　Individual, 180, 180
Lobster Tails, Deviled, 134, 135

M

Manicotti, Spinach Pesto, 76
Marshmallows
　Layered Mint-Chocolate Fudge,
　　216, 217
　Santa Grahams, 250, 250
Marzipan-Stuffed Apricots in
　Chocolate, 228
Meat. See Beef; Lamb; Pork
Meatballs, Creole, 21
Mediterranean Fennel Salad, 156,
　157
Menu ideas
　Casual Holiday Get-Togethers,
　　72
　Elegant Holiday Menus, 108
Meringues, Mint-Kissed, 210, 211
Mint-Chocolate Fudge, Layered,
　216, 217
Mint-Kissed Meringues, 210, 211
Mitten, Giant Snowy, 246, 247
Mocha Truffle Cheesecake, 190,
　191
Mousse, Cranberry, 197
Muffin Mix, Merry Ginger, 232,
　233
Muffins, Cranberry Upside-Down,
　48, 49
Muffins, Parmesan-Herb, 50

Mushroom(s)
　-Brandy Sauce, Peppered Steak
　　with, 109
　Make-Ahead Scrambled Eggs,
　　83
　Seafood and Cheese Brunch
　　Bake, 100, 101
　Slow-Cooked Beef Burgundy, 73
　Teriyaki Seafood-Stuffed, 30, 31
　Turkey with Italian Roasted
　　Vegetables, 98
　Winter Portobello Ratatouille,
　　105
Mustard
　Cranberry, 240, 240
　Dijon Sauce, 133
　Honey-, Dilled Brussels Sprouts,
　　141
　Honey-, Roasted Chicken and
　　Squash, 126, 127

N

Nutrition information, 262–63
Nuts. See also Almond(s); Pecan(s);
　Walnut(s)
　Chocolate-Cashew Pie, 176
　Chocolate-Toffee Bars, 207
　Holiday Focaccia, 63
　Holiday Spiced, 242, 243
　Nutty Holiday Popcorn, 43
　Roast Goose with Chestnut-
　　Prune Stuffing, 132

O

Olive and Goat Cheese Phyllo
　Purses, 42
Onion, Caramelized, and Beef
　Tenderloin Sandwiches, 22
Onion Biscuits, Crispy, 58
Onion-Garlic Loaf, 62
Orange(s)
　Crème Dessert with Ruby
　　Cranberry Sauce, 182
　-Fennel Halibut, Roasted, with
　　Dijon Sauce, 133, 133
　Jiggle Bell Salad, 160, 161
　-Spice Coffee Mix, 234
　Spritz, 206
Oyster Stew, Festive, 102

P

Parmesan-Dill Popovers, 55
Parmesan-Garlic Butter Green
　Beans, 145, 145
Parmesan-Herb Muffins, 50

Pasta
　Fried Ravioli with Tomato Sauce,
　　36, 37
　Herbed Alfredo Sauce over
　　Linguine, 104, 104
　Pizza Lasagna, 84, 85
　Spinach Pesto Manicotti, 76
Pastrami and Pepper Roll-ups, 19
Peach-Cranberry Gingerbread
　Trifle, 192
Peanut butter
　Almost-Instant Buckeyes, 222,
　　223
　Chicken Peanut Kabobs, 28, 29
Peanuts
　Nutty Holiday Popcorn, 43
Pear(s)
　Chutney, Spiced, 235
　Winter Fruit Salad, 159
Peas
　Garden, Potatoes Alfredo with,
　　152
　Green, Tarragon, 110, 146
　Honey-Mustard Roasted Chicken
　　and Squash, 126, 127
Pecan(s)
　Caramel Sauce, 241
　Eggnog Ice Cream Dessert, 184
　Holiday Spiced Nuts, 242, 243
　Savory Nutty Crescents, 46
　Sweet Nutcracker Braid, 68, 69
Pepper-Crusted Prime Rib with
　Zinfandel Sauce, 112, 113
Peppered Beef Tenderloin with
　Wine Sauce, 111
Peppered Steak with Brandy-
　Mushroom Sauce, 109
Peppermint-Bark Hearts, 220, 221
Peppermint-Topped Brownie
　Dessert, Creamy, 194, 195
Pepper(s)
　Bagel 'n Brie Brunch Strata, 137
　Chile Aïoli, 34, 35
　Chili Cheese Dip and Potato
　　Wedges, 20, 20
　Chipotle-Black Bean Chili, 103
　Festive Coleslaw with Citrus
　　Vinaigrette, 162
　Italian Mixed Green Salad, 110,
　　155
　Mediterranean Fennel Salad, 156,
　　157
　and Pastrami Roll-ups, 19
　and Pesto-Stuffed Leg of Lamb,
　　124, 125

Pesto
    Mini Pizzas, 38
    and Pepper-Stuffed Leg of Lamb,
        124, *125*
    Spinach Manicotti, 76
Phyllo Purses, Goat Cheese and
    Olive, 42
Pie. *See also* Tarts
    Chocolate-Cashew, 176
    Cranberry-Apple Streusel, *174*,
        175
    Strawberry-Fudge, 177
Pineapple-Orange Glazed Ham, 117
Pizza Lasagna, 84, *85*
Pizzas, Mini, 38
Polenta Stars, Baked Herbed, 154
Pomegranate-Champagne
    Vinaigrette, Winter Greens
    with, 158
Pomegranate Tartlets, 181
Popcorn, Nutty Holiday, 43
Popovers, Dill-Parmesan, 55
Pops, Christmas Tree Candy, *224*,
    225
Pork
    Baked Ham with Zesty
        Cranberry Sauce, 116
    Beef, Bacon and Barley Soup, 80
    Chicken and Sausage Stew, 87
    Chicken Peanut Kabobs, 28, *29*
    Chops, Apple-Glazed, with Sage-
        Apple Stuffing, 123
    Chops and Vegetables, Oven-
        Roasted, 78, *79*
    Glazed Crown Roast with
        Cranberry-Cornbread Stuffing,
        118, *119*
    Make-Ahead Scrambled Eggs, 83
    Pastrami and Pepper Roll-ups, 19
    Pineapple-Orange Glazed Ham,
        117
    Roast, Fennel-Garlic, 122
    Saucy Sausage Medallions, 26
    Sausage and Egg Brunch Bake, 82
    Tenderloin, Spice and Herb-
        Roasted, 120, *121*
    Tenderloin Crostini, 24, *25*
    Turkey and Ham Crescent Braid,
        94, *95*
Potato(es)
    Alfredo with Garden Peas, 152
    Beef, Bacon and Barley Soup, 80
    Festive Oyster Stew, 102
    Red, Garlic Smashed, 153, *153*
    Sausage and Egg Brunch Bake, 82

    Skillet Chicken and Winter
        Vegetables, 90, *91*
    and Smoky Cheese Bake, 151
    Sweet, with Apples and Onions,
        147
    Three-, Gratin, 148, *149*
    Turkey with Italian Roasted
        Vegetables, 98
    Wedges, Chili Cheese Dip and,
        20, *20*
Poultry. *See also* Chicken; Turkey
    Cherry-Balsamic Cornish Hen
        with Rice, 130, *131*
    Roast Goose with Chestnut-
        Prune Stuffing, 132
Pretzel(s)
    Santa's Reindeer Cookies, 252,
        253
    Wreaths, *248*, 249
Pudding, Eggnog Bread, with
    Cherry-Bourbon Sauce, 193

Q
Quesadillas, Turkey-Cranberry, 27
Quiches, Mini Asian Crab, 32

R
Raspberry-White Chocolate Bars,
    208, 209
Raspberry Cream Heart, 185
Ratatouille, Winter Portobello, 105
Ravioli, Fried, with Tomato Sauce,
    36, 37
Rice, Cherry-Balsamic Cornish Hen
    with, 130, *131*
Rolls, Overnight Caramel-Apple,
    56, *57*
Rum Sauce, Hot Buttered, 239, *239*

S
Salad
    Festive Coleslaw with Citrus
        Vinaigrette, 162
    Italian Mixed Green, *110*, 155
    Jiggle Bell, *160*, 161
    Winter Fruit, 159
    Winter Greens with
        Pomegranate-Champagne
        Vinaigrette, 158
Salmon, Italian Roasted, 136
Salmon, Smoked, on Endive, 33
Salsa and Black Bean Dip, *236*, 236
Sandwiches, bite-sized
    Beef Crostini with Caper
        Mayonnaise, 18

    Beef Tenderloin and Caramelized
        Onion, 22
    Pork Tenderloin Crostini, 24, *25*
    Turkey-Cranberry Quesadillas, 27
Santa Grahams, 250, *250*
Santa's Reindeer Cookies, 252, *253*
Sauce
    Caramel Pecan, 241
    Gravy, 128–29
    Hot Buttered Rum, 239, *239*
    Tomato, Fried Ravioli with, *36*, 37
Sauce, dipping
    Aïoli Dip, 74, *75*
    Curry Dip, 74, *75*
    Horseradish Sauce, 74, *75*
    Steak Sauce, 74, *75*
Sausage
    and Chicken Stew, 87
    and Egg Brunch Bake, 82
    Medallions, Saucy, 26
Scones, Apple-Ginger, 52, *53*
Scones, Savory Cheese and
    Scallion, 54
Seafood. *See* Fish; Shellfish
Shellfish
    Asian Mini Quiches, 32
    Cilantro-Lime Shrimp with Chile
        Aïoli, 34, *35*
    Deviled Lobster Tails, 134, *135*
    Festive Oyster Stew, 102
    Seafood and Cheese Brunch
        Bake, 100, *101*
    Teriyaki Seafood-Stuffed
        Mushrooms, 30, *31*
Shrimp
    Cilantro-Lime, with Chile Aïoli,
        34, *35*
    Seafood and Cheese Brunch
        Bake, 100, *101*
Side dishes
    Almond Baby Carrots, 142, *143*
    Baked Brandied Cranberries,
        163
    Baked Herbed Polenta Stars,
        154
    Broccoli with Walnut-Garlic
        Butter, 140
    Festive Coleslaw with Citrus
        Vinaigrette, 162
    Garlic Smashed Red Potatoes,
        153, *153*
    Honey-Mustard Dilled Brussels
        Sprouts, 141
    Italian Mixed Green Salad, *110*,
        155

Side dishes (*continued*)
  Jiggle Bell Salad, 160, 161
  Mediterranean Fennel Salad, 156, 157
  Parmesan-Garlic Butter Green Beans, 145, 145
  Potatoes Alfredo with Garden Peas, 152
  Smoky Cheese and Potato Bake, 151
  Sweet Potatoes with Apples and Onions, 147
  Tarragon Green Peas, 110, 146
  Three-Potato Gratin, 148, 149
  Winter Fruit Salad, 159
  Winter Greens with Pomegranate-Champagne Vinaigrette, 158
Smoked Salmon on Endive, 33
Smoky Cheese and Potato Bake, 151
Snacks. *See* Starters and snacks
Snowman Faces, 254, 255
Snowmen, Craft Dough, 251
Soups. *See also* Stews
  Beef, Bacon and Barley, 80
  Creamy Chicken-Vegetable Chowder, 86
Spice and Herb-Roasted Pork Tenderloin, 120, 121
Spiced Chocolate Crinkles, 202
Spiced Cider Cheesecake, 188–89
Spiced Nuts, Holiday, 242, 243
Spiced Pear Chutney, 235
Spiced Walnut Brittle, 218
Spinach Pesto Manicotti, 76
Spread, Cherry-Cheese, 40, 41
Squash
  Honey-Mustard Roasted Chicken and, 126, 127
  Winter Portobello Ratatouille, 105
Starters and snacks
  Asian Crab Mini Quiches, 32
  Beef Crostini with Caper Mayonnaise, 18
  Beef Tenderloin and Caramelized Onion Sandwiches, 22
  Cherry-Cheese Spread, 40, 41
  Chicken Peanut Kabobs, 28, 29
  Chili Cheese Dip and Potato Wedges, 20, 20
  Cilantro-Lime Shrimp with Chile Aïoli, 34, 35
  Creole Meatballs, 21

Fried Ravioli with Tomato Sauce, 36, 37
Goat Cheese and Olive Phyllo Purses, 42
Holiday Spiced Nuts, 242, 243
Mini Pizzas, 38
Nutty Holiday Popcorn, 43
Pastrami and Pepper Roll-Ups, 19
Pork Tenderloin Crostini, 24, 25
Saucy Sausage Medallions, 26
Smoked Salmon on Endive, 33
Teriyaki Seafood-Stuffed Mushrooms, 30, 31
Turkey-Cranberry Quesadillas, 27
Stews
  Chicken and Sausage, 87
  Chipotle-Black Bean Chili, 103
  Festive Oyster, 102
  Slow-Cooked Beef Burgundy, 73
Strawberry-Fudge Pie, 177
Sugar Cone Trees, 256, 256
Sweet Potatoes
  with Apples and Onions, 147
  Three-Potato Gratin, 148, 149

T

Table decorations
  candle and fruit centerpiece, 51, 51
  candle and sugar centerpiece, 36, 36
  candy cane place settings, 249, 249
  floating candle vases, 129, 129
  individual candle place settings, 23, 23
  miniature decorated trees, 77, 77
  ornament-wrapped napkins, 169, 169
  pinecone place settings, 213, 213
  vellum luminaria, 150, 150
Tarragon Green Peas, 110, 146
Tarts
  Individual Lemon-Lime Cream, 180, 180
  Pomegranate Tartlets, 181
  Triple-Chocolate Truffle Trees, 178, 179
Teriyaki Seafood-Stuffed Mushrooms, 30, 31
Three-Cheese Crescent Pinwheels, 47
Three-Potato Gratin, 148, 149

Tomato(es)
  Chipotle-Black Bean Chili, 103
  Italian Mixed Green Salad, 110, 155
  Mini Pizzas, 38
  Party Chicken Cacciatore, 88, 89
  Sauce, Fried Ravioli with, 36, 37
  Winter Portobello Ratatouille, 105
Tortillas
  Overnight Chicken Enchilada Bake, 93
  Turkey-Cranberry Quesadillas, 27
Train, Candy, 257
Trifle, Cranberry-Peach Gingerbread, 192
Turkey
  Breast, Lemon and Herb-Roasted, 96, 97
  -Cranberry Quesadillas, 27
  and Ham Crescent Braid, 94, 95
  with Italian Roasted Vegetables, 98
  Stuffed Roast, and Gravy, 128–29

V

Vegetable(s). *See also* specific vegetables
  Crescent Chicken Newburg, 92
  Italian Roasted, Turkey with, 98
  Oven-Roasted Pork Chops and, 78, 79

W

Walnut(s)
  Brittle, Spiced, 218
  -Cranberry White Fudge, 219
  -Garlic Butter, Broccoli with, 140
  toasting, 218
White Chocolate-Iced Cranberry Bread, 64, 65
White Chocolate-Raspberry Bars, 208, 209
Wine Sauce, Peppered Beef Tenderloin with, 111
Winter Fruit Salad, 159

Z

Zinfandel Sauce, Pepper-Crusted Prime Rib with, 112, 113
Zucchini
  Winter Portobello Ratatouille, 105

Metric Conversion Guide

volume

U.S. UNITS	CANADIAN METRIC	AUSTRALIAN METRIC
1/4 teaspoon	1 ml	1 ml
1/2 teaspoon	2 ml	2 ml
1 teaspoon	5 ml	5 ml
1 tablespoon	15 ml	20 ml
1/4 cup	50 ml	60 ml
1/3 cup	75 ml	80 ml
1/2 cup	125 ml	125 ml
2/3 cup	150 ml	170 ml
3/4 cup	175 ml	190 ml
1 cup	250 ml	250 ml
1 quart	1 liter	1 liter
1 1/2 quarts	1.5 liters	1.5 liters
2 quarts	2 liters	2 liters
2 1/2 quarts	2.5 liters	2.5 liters
3 quarts	3 liters	3 liters
4 quarts	4 liters	4 liters

weight

U.S. UNITS	CANADIAN METRIC	AUSTRALIAN METRIC
1 ounce	30 grams	30 grams
2 ounces	55 grams	60 grams
3 ounces	85 grams	90 grams
4 ounces (1/4 pound)	115 grams	125 grams
8 ounces (1/2 pound)	225 grams	225 grams
16 ounces (1 pound)	455 grams	500 grams
1 pound	455 grams	1/2 kilogram

measurements

INCHES	CENTIMETERS
1	2.5
2	5.0
3	7.5
4	10.0
5	12.5
6	15.0
7	17.5
8	20.5
9	23.0
10	25.5
11	28.0
12	30.5
13	33.0

temperatures

FAHRENHEIT	CELSIUS
32°	0°
212°	100°
250°	120°
275°	140°
300°	150°
325°	160°
350°	180°
375°	190°
400°	200°
425°	220°
450°	230°
475°	240°
500°	260°

Note: The recipes in this cookbook have not been developed or tested using metric measures. When converting recipes to metric, some variations in quality may be noted.

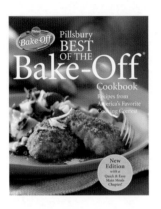

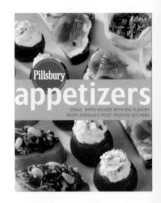

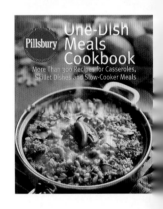

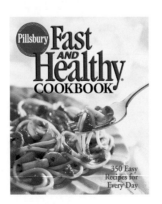